Australian Literature

Paradigms, Praxis and Theory

Australian Literature

Paradigms, Praxis and Theory

Edited by

Shiv Govind Puri

ATLANTIC

PUBLISHERS & DISTRIBUTORS (P) LTD

Published by
ATLANTIC
PUBLISHERS & DISTRIBUTORS (P) LTD
7/22, Ansari Road, Darya Ganj, New Delhi-110002
Phones : +91-11-40775252, 23273880, 23275880, 23280451
Fax : +91-11-23285873
Web : www.atlanticbooks.com
E-mail : orders@atlanticbooks.com

Branch Office
5, Nallathambi Street, Wallajah Road, Chennai-600002
Phones : +91-44-64611085, 32413319
E-mail : chennai@atlanticbooks.com

Reprint 2018

Printed in India at Nice Printing Press, A-33/3A, Site-IV,
Industrial Area, Sahibabad, Ghaziabad, U.P.

Preface

Australian literature has a rich tradition of its developments, explorations and achievements. Similarly, Australian literature has also various perspectives which impacted the great luminaries such as Judith Wright, A.D. Hope, James McAuley, Peter Porter, Sally Morgan, Kevin Hart and Patrick White who have contributed immensely to the growth and development of Australian literature. As compared with Indian English literature and British literature, Australian literature has had a short span of journey so far because of the late inception of its literary developments. However, in a very short period of time, it has imbibed the richness and glory of literary ambience. The contemporary writers of the region have covered various issues which have been much prevalent over a period of time.

Australia is a multicultural, multiethnic country which gives this nation a distinct national identity. Australia is changing in the positive direction and I am very hopeful that the present book would adopt and explore all the changes and challenges that have made the country proud. Australian literature is a new emerging area of study not only in Australia but in the whole world. Contemporary writers of the Australian literature have focused their writings on nature, culture and identity which have created a space for researchers and the intellectuals to work in this area.

An attempt has been made to put all possible genres together which reflect the multitude colours of this part of the land. The book will be useful for the students, teachers and researchers of Australian literature. The themes of aboriginality, migration and national identity explored in Australian literature will be useful for researchers in diasporic literature.

I wish to express my deep sense of gratitude to all contributors who have supported this academic venture. I wish to extend my thanks to Prof. Nishi Pandey, Prof. V.P. Singh and Prof. Ranu Uniyal—all from University of Lucknow for their suggestions and support given to me from time to time. Last, but not least, the publisher of this book also deserves my special thanks and admiration for bringing out this book so nicely and in time.

Shiv Govind Puri

Introduction

José Carlos in his paper, "Les Murray: Sensing Poetry through Place" has discussed the history and landscape of Australia. Jose has also discussed the poet Les Murray's personal life, parentage and relationships. He has marked the contribution of Judith Wright, Hopkins and Kenneth Slessor who have given their literary inputs in the development of Australian literature. Murray's tensions about such rural/urban life, independent/non-independent means of expression, the ordinary/the elite academicizing the natural and spacious, are reflected in his poetry. Jose's article has been divided into three parts; The Poet, The Background, Time and Poetry, and Location through which he has covered the creative spirit/vision of Murray.

Deepak Kumar Singh in his paper, "Autobiographical Underpinnings in Patrick White's *The Solid Mandala*" studies one novel, namely *The Solid Mandala* and depicts the black comedy and kitchen-sink realism. He has also analyzed the search for spiritual and emotional wholeness, the holocaust and an impinging ethos of materialism.

Sudhir K. Arora's paper, "Seeking an Answer for the Honour of the Fallen: Ada Cambridge's Feminist Issues" offers a study of the freedom of Australian women from the fetters of the masculine domination for which he has focused on Ada Cambridge's four poems from her poetry collection *Unspoken Thoughts*.

Jaydeep Sarangi in his paper, "Two Nimbin (Australia) Poets: An Overview of Rob Harle and Nathalie Buckland" deals with life and career of Rob Harle. He has also focused on the writer's literary contribution to the country, Australia. Rob Harle's beautiful expressions highlight human universe constantly getting challenged by the digital universe. Jaydeep Sarangi's other deliberation is in "Jaydeep Sarangi in Conversation with Michelle Cahill", which deals with the life of Goan-Anglo-Indian writer who lives in Sydney, Australia. It was an interface conversation which focuses mainly on Michelle's writing journey, deliberation of thoughts and opinions formed in Australia with the texture of Indian trajectory.

Darkhasha Azhar's paper, "Kevin Gilbert's Aboriginal Verse: An Epitome of Uniform Justice" offers a study of aboriginal sentiments. She deals with the mixture of two cultures developing in the life of Gilbert under the white and black parentage and provides an investigation of relationships.

Neeta's paper, "Reflections on Eco-criticism in Judith Wright's Poetry" presents an eco-critical study of Judith Wright's poetry through narrative discourses. She has also elaborated socio-political conditions of the period through her writings.

Meenu Dubey's paper, "*The Waste Land* and *The Living and the Dead*: A Utopian Perspective" offers a study of modern man's life and devastating predicament. She has also underscored various permutations of philosophical conditioning analyzing the connections between physical phase of life as well as the spiritual phase.

Arun Kumar Yadav's paper, "Emergence of Laura in Patrick White's *Voss*" is a study of Australian society during the 1840s. Yadav has also endeavoured to depict the sexuate relationships of Australian colonial period.

Neha Arora's paper, "The Fourth World Shouts Back...'We Have Arrived'" conceptualizes in reversing the centre-margin relationship between the colonizer and the colonized. The paper also focuses on marginalizing the indigenous people.

V. Kundhavi in her paper, "Counter History and Race War Discourse of the Stolen Generations in Doris Pilkington's *Follow the Rabbit-Proof Fence*" depicts the discourse of race war that emerged in the 17th century and replaced old historiography. She has justified her views with regard to war and race conceptualizing Foucault's discourse theory. She has exhaustively quoted/explored her views on cultural space and identity. She also interprets the theories of feminist authors who have made a niche for themselves. She has given enough space to every character to develop their personality in the social as well as cultural conditioning.

Ravindra Kumar in his paper, "Rebellion against the Culture of Stoicism and the Land in A.D. Hope's 'Australia'" explores the sense of emotional turmoil, loss and anguish due to cultural crossovers in his works. His characters/narratives establish their identity with the traditional outlook.

Kartika Prakash Dubey in her paper, "Judith Wright: Perspective from Nation, Love and Death" presents concern of the writer about the roots and indigenous paradigms of the land. There are discussions of elements like human relationships, pollution, dehumanization and cultural ghettoes in her work.

Arzoo Naqvi in her paper, "Writing the Self: Australian Women Autobiographies" has developed a discourse based on the literature and settlement of aboriginal culture. She has also aptly described the clash of two cultures suppressing the human relationships.

Jaba Kusum Singh in her paper, "Ada Cambridge's *An Answer*: A Re-Study of Post-Colonialism and an Australian Poem" creates a space for memorization of the oral script and dialogue with special reference to prehistoric period. She has also developed her arguments on classical texts like Homer's *Iliad* and *Odyssey* which fillip the sanctity of the perennial developments.

Dhananjay Kumar Singh in his article, "The Daring Exploits of Mr. Johann Ulrich Voss" has created the whole idea of nation like Australia as a 'miserable country' according to Mrs. Bonner who is a naturalized citizen of Australia. Journey is another theme that has been taken up in this article. Singh has exhaustively quoted ideas/expressions of the narratives through a number of novels including Joseph Conrad's *Heart of Darkness*, and Patrick White's *Voss*. He has also presented the history of Britain and America. In the background of his arguments he has taken some help from the African literatures as well. He has defined the settlers' life as well as migrants' life. Singh has justified through his reflective arguments that Patrick White remains one of the best and most interesting authors of his generation.

Shiv Govind Puri

Contents

Contributors

Arun Kumar Yadav, Research Scholar, Dept. of English and MEL, University of Lucknow, Uttar Pradesh

Arzoo Naqvi, Research Scholar, Dept. of English, Banaras Hindu University, Varanasi, Uttar Pradesh

Darkhasha Azhar, Assistant Professor, Dept. of English, Govt. P.G. College, Bisalpur, Madhya Pradesh

Deepak Kumar Singh, Assistant Professor, Dept. of English, D.A.V. College, Lucknow, Uttar Pradesh

Dhananjay Kumar Singh, Assistant Professor, T.B.S. College, Tundla, Uttar Pradesh

Jaba Kusum Singh, Associate Professor, Dept. of English, Upadhi Mahavidyalaya, Pilibhit, Uttar Pradesh

Jaydeep Sarangi, Associate Professor, Dept. of English, Jogesh Chandra Chaudhury College (Calcutta University), Kolkata, West Bengal

José Carlos, Dept. of Philology, Faculty of Humanities, Universidad de Almeria/University of Almeria, Spain

Kartika Prakash Dubey, Faculty Member, TERI University, New Delhi

Meenu Dubey, Associate Professor, Dept. of English, Raja Mohan Girls P.G. College, Faizabad, Uttar Pradesh

Neeta, Associate Professor, Dept. of English, S.V. College, Aligarh, Uttar Pradesh

Neha Arora, Assistant Professor, Dept. of English, Central University of Rajasthan, Jaipur, Rajasthan

Ravindra Kumar, Assistant Professor, Dept. of English, C.C.S. University, Meerut, Uttar Pradesh

Sudhir K. Arora, Assistant Professor, Dept. of English, Maharaja Harischandra College, Moradabad, Uttar Pradesh

V. Kundhavi, Associate Professor, Dept. of English, Government Arts College (Autonomous), Salem, Tamil Nadu

1

Les Murray: Sensing Poetry through Place

José Carlos

1. The Poet: The Background

"On his forty acre farm Les Murray is surrounded by the geography, history and landscape of life. Everywhere about the talismans of his art, lines from his poems." Those were the words of Graeme Kinross-Smith (1980: 39) when trying to establish a profile of the poet Les Murray linked to the image of farms in his poetry. The thing is that his ancestors the Murrays, came to the Manning Valley of Australia as squatters in 1845, but his grandfather, John Murray settled in this valley at Bunyah, the central coast hinterland, in 1870. Beyond that is the mid north coast of New South Wales, Les Murray's region. This is Murray's *Omphalos*, his gravity centre. He grew up on a farm where his father was the tenant of his grandfather's dairying 140 acres. His childhood was very isolated and it was certainly a hard background but one that entrenched upon him a love of the landscape and people of rural Australia. He was the only child of Cecil Murray and his wife Miriam (née Arnall), dairy farmers, and he met very few other kids until he was nine years old. He went to Bulby Brush School, a three and half miles walk over the mountain, but when his mother died in 1951, he had no schooling for a year and then went to Nabiac Central School, where he was among 150 other children. It seems that it was in that time that he came to a vague conclusion that he wanted to be a writer. From that time he recalled how his English teacher, Mr McLaughlin introduced the students to T.S. Eliot and Gerard Manley Hopkins, and how Hopkins showed him that language could be exciting, alive and about relevant things. Before Murray had seen poetry as something in an archaic language and that even could have died out. When commentaries about Australian poetry appeared though the names like R.D. Fitzgerald, Kenneth Slessor or Judith Wright, he realized that modern poetry was written is Australia too. In 1955-56, he completed two further years of schooling as at Taree High, there Murray's keen intellect, corpulence, and lack of social poise made him the focus of sustained bullying, an experience that deeply marked him. It seems that it was round 1956 when the poet started writing ten poems and sent them to the *Bulletin* and we know that they bounced them.

In 1957, he tried to join the Air Force and was rejected. Then he went to Sydney University on a Commonwealth scholarship, there he discovered the Fisher Library, a place he fell in love with and where he taught himself several languages using the University Teach Yourself books. At Sydney University he spent four years (1957-60) without graduating. Later he worked for the Telephone Accounts Branch of the PMG (The Australian Government Postmaster-General's Department) and other jobs with not very good experiences. In those years, he hitch-hiked Australia and among other experiences he took part in a play sponsored by the Department of German at the University of Sydney. It was crucial because at that time he met Valerie Morelli who was wardrobe mistress for this play. She came from a family of emigrants, in fact, she was born in Hungary and raised in Switzerland and finally her family migrated to Australia when she was ten years old. Les Murray married her in September 1962. They settled in an inner western suburb of Sydney, Glebe, but in the following year they moved to Canberra, where he found a job in the Translation Unit at the Australian National University. It was an interesting job because in spite of the fact that the material was mostly scientific and technical, he was satisfied with the particulars of language and the possibilities of information. In 1964, he became a Catholic, probably under the influence of his reverence for the sanctity of life though the small wonders of existence as well as under the stimulus of his wife's Catholicism. In 1965, the poet was invited to Cardiff for the British Arts Festival Poetry Conference, this proved influential as in 1967 he quit his job in Canberra and went to Cardiff. His family (Valerie and their two children) followed later and they stayed there for fourteen months. It proved to be a very nice experience and a kind of Australian grand tour.

The Murray family came back to Australia in 1968. The poet went back to Sydney University, there he studied German and Linguistics and took out his degree. He was promised a Commonwealth grant and with this in mind he went to live to Canberra where he set up and started to compile a book of translations of Aboriginal poems, something he had looked forward to doing. The fact is that the promises were not fulfilled and he began working as a clerk in the Prime Minister's Department and later at the Department of Education and Science in Sydney. It was the kind of undemanding and boring work he did not like, but luckily things were changing and his poetry became better known. In 1965, he published his first book *The Ilex Tree*, it was a volume shared with his fellow Sydney poet and friend Geoffrey Lehmann. It showed poems such as "Noonday Axeman", "Driving through Sawmill Towns" or "The Widower in the Country" and put on view Murray's sense of people and place. In 1969, *The Weatherboard Cathedral*, his second collection, was minted. It was a time in which awards and formal recognitions appeared, such as *The Commonwealth Literary Fund* (1968) or the winnerof the *Poetry Section of the Captain Cook Bicentenary Literary Competition* (1970). They and subsequent fellowships acted as wake-up calls and appetizers for Murray literary career.

Later he reached a situation in which he could live in a sound security without relying on literary fellowships. It was the poet, novelist and writer of short fiction Graeme Kinross-Smith (1980: 46) the one that mentioned that Murray's writing and thinking "has been fertilized by a number of quite disparate writers" among them the Australians Kenneth Slessor and Douglas Stewart, among the classics, Virgil, Hesiod, Horace,

Pindar, from them he seems to appreciate "their extreme economy, skill and tact with words". He equally sees the echoes of The American poet Robinson Jeffers and the presence of many German poets and a lot of Celts. In fact a good evidence of this is his appearance in a special Gaelic issue of Poetry Australia or poems like "The Gaelic Long Tunes".

He is without doubt a prolific writer, apart from the aforementioned titles, he published *Poems Against Economics* (1972), *Lunch and Counter Lunch* (1974), *The Vernacular Republic* (1976), *Ethnic Radio* (1977) and numberless reviews and articles in *The Bulletin, Australian Quarterly, The Sydney Morning Herald*...many of them appeared in 1978 under the title of *The Peasant Mandarin*, mostly a collection of reflections sometimes earthbound and claiming for renovation and sometimes weird and beyond the sensory.

The 1980s was a time for recognition and with it came a greater international acclaim. It was a time for plenty of published poetry, *Equanimities* (1982), *The People's Otherworld* (1983), *The Daylight Noon* (1987) or *The Dog Fox Field* (1990). In the mid of the eighties he and his family left Sydney to live at Bunyah, the place of his ancestors, there he has lived ever since. This decade also represented appraise at home through the awarding of several prizes and in 1989 his contribution to Australian Literature was distinguished with the award of an Order of Australia.

However, if the eighties represented happy times, the nineties of the twentieth century were marked through illness (chronic depression and liver abscess) and public controversies (among other, Murray and his supporters alleged political bias in the distribution of funds from the Literature Board of the Australia Council). Fortunately, it did not mean the stopping of poetic creativity as he continued producing other volumes of poetry. In 1991 his Barbara Ramsden award winning *Collected Poems* appeared. 1992 saw the publishing of *Translations from the Natural World*, and other work, *Subhuman Redneck Poems* won the Kenneth Slessor Prize, the C.J. Dennis Prize as well as the prestigious T.S. Eliot Award. It was illness and the narrow escaping of death the experiences that left an inprint upon the semi-autobiographical verse novel *Fredy Neptune* (1998) and the volume of verse *Conscious and Verbal* (1999). Prose has also been omnipresent in his output through essays and criticism, among the most remarkable collections we can name *Persistence in Folly* (1984), *Blocks and Tackles* (1990), *A Working Forest* (1997), and *The Quality of Sprawl: Thoughts about Australia* (1999).

The new millennium has represented a continuity frame for a poet of his age, though much of it reinforces the autobiographical element and Australian rural values. After *An Absolutely Ordinary Rainbow* (2000), other works followed, thus *Learning Human, Selected Poems* (2001), *Poems the Size of Photographs* (2002), *New Collected Poems* (2003), *The Biplane Houses* (2007), *Taller When Prone* (2010), *Killing the Black Dog: A Memoir of Depression* (2011) and *New Selected Poems* (2014). In them one can clearly appreciate his opposition to the intellectual cliques and snobbery stemming from the cities. For Murray those influences, tensions and oppositions such as rural/urban life, independent/non-independent means of expression, the ordinary/the elite, academicizing/the natural and spacious, are part of our world. Nevertheless, these disputes do not prevent him from celebrating God and creation with equal facility and enthusiasm. In them, as Peter Porter remarked, Murray shows "that nothing is certain and faces with wit and invention the mystery to come" (15 March 2003). Les Murray is often called Australia's Bush-bard and media have referred to him as Australia's 'unofficial poet laureate' and according to Lawrence Bourke (1992), he has described himself in a half-joking way, as the last of the Jindyworobaks, an Australian literary movement whose members, mostly white, intended to prop up indigenous Australian ideas and customs, specially through poetry.[1] The poet has been several times in the pools for the Nobel Prize, and in 2007, Dan Chiasson wrote in *The New*

1. According to Gary Clark (2003) and Brian Elliot (1979), The word "jindyworobak" is Australian Aboriginal-meaning "to annex or join." It was the meeting or hybridization of white and black culture that was central to the aesthetic and philosophical disposition of the movement's spokesman and founder Rex Ingamells (1938).

Yorker that he was "routinely mentioned among the three or four leading English-language poets" (11 June 2007).

2. Time and Poetry

We know that poetry has run through history, civilization and languages. It is a song, a story and true and alive human memory, because we essentially remember something that in some moment was meaningful to us. It was Robert Graves the one that said that for the poet, poetry can have two essential meanings: "the unforeseen fusion in his mind of apparently contradictory emotional ideas" or like "the more-or-less deliberate attempt, with the help of a rhythmic mesmerism, to impose an illusion of actual experience on the minds of others". According to it poetry can be envisioned as a construction of thought and thought can be intended as a construction of poetry. It is almost like a theory of human communication based on and exemplified through the factual virtuality of verse.

Subsequently, we can speak on truth in poetry in the traditional sense of the "adequatio rei"—adequacy to the thing (matter)—. This is liable with the condition of moving from the ontological to the phenomenological and at the same time substituting "thing" for "experience". A poem describes the undergone experience in terms of something lived, expresses the existence in its own language. If we compare poetry with the novel, we can appreciate that poetry has not got a kind of dependency upon the fictitious element, as happens with the novel, and, of course, owes nothing to the imaginary constituent. The poets' imagination is completely verbal and the word can be understood as a capacity for the invention of something that is non real. This might explain why many poets decide to write narrative, they choose the fantastic genre, because the fantastic genre carries more poeticity. According to János S. Petöfi and Terry Olivi (1994: 200) "a verbally initiated non-verbal verbal process."

On equal terms we must account for the fact that the fantastic component is a referential deviation, poetry, on the other hand is a linguistic one. The fantastic component changes things, in poetry the deviation is of linguistic nature. That is why the poet is, above all an amalgamate or a joiner of two qualities: linguistic creativity and sensitiveness. It is equally true that there is no symmetry principle in mingling, but the two ingredients are necessary for the poet, not with the reader, he/she only needs sensitiveness. Poetry is also a mirroring phenomenon of inwardness made possible through the contemplation of the outer world. It is a creation that allows to unveil the anthropological sense that dwells in man/woman through poetic figuring.

The world of poetry is a human world and poetry is the discourse that describes man/woman through his/her inner truth. It is the authentic phenomenology. We could even wonder if it goes a step beyond phenomenology. Philosophical phenomenology, as we know, tries to describe and so interpret reality in a faithful way, but poetry aspire not only to watch the world, but also to live it. It is a kind of watching through living or living through watching experience. As it happens with physicists poets seem to be searching for truth, though it is obvious that each one defines and tries to interpret truth according to his/her own system of rules. The parallel is also there when we appreciate that in any field the faculty of creation has an emotional dimension and the way and idea arises is not usually objective.

The classic conception of writing, as it happens with reading, implies the awareness of time and its limits. Poetry is the metronome and the poet and reader the performers. The word is the world beat that acquires sense though association. By reading, what we simply do is to restore the beauty or truth that hangs from time. On the other hand, poetry is neither trustful nor truthful in the intellectual sense, nor it is beautiful as craftwork, quite on the contrary, because it gives expression in a beautiful way it is precisely why it captures truth.

Poetry has also been interpreted as disclosure, but paradoxically it also uncovers those spaces of lack. We read because we have no answers, no questions, no time, no words and it is because of it that poetry reveals itself as promise. A poem is basically a text as a revelation; it is a stepping stone for knowledge. In fact, when we read we attempt a binding process to connect knowledge through time. We are builders of a time, our own time, but time is not just time, it is place, data, music....

We know now, as the physicists have already explained that time is place and vice versa, but the poets knew it long time ago, they knew that the space-time fusion was possible thanks to beauty.

Poetry is also a linguistic operation built upon imperfect materials but with the aspiration to go farther beyond words or outside them. Poetry means more than it says, we could even say that the true plasticity of poetry lies beyond words, and clearly beyond the realm of writing. It is certainly a *plus dicendi*, subsequently in the building work of poetry words produce realities, fence silence margins in and illuminate the limits of impossibility.

Words do suggest and mean more in a poem that in an ordinary text and every poem is symbolic as in the symbolic designation, the intuitive designation of the symbol is essential. A poem is not just neither a linguistic construction nor a space to light meaning, the poem is, as I.A. Richards, T.S. Eliot, G. Leopardi or Joan Ferraté mentioned, 'in itself'.

To describe the notion of place in Les Murray from a phenomenological point of view is first and foremost to pay attention to the poetics of place. We know that place as well as time is one of the two basic coordinates involved in the building of the literary imagination. The mythical-spatial constitution that we associate with a literary text is grounded and projected in a design that corresponds to the writing of the text. In other words, it is based upon the meaning of the expressive material used. In fact, it was the philosopher Immanuel Kant (1724-1804) the one that put forward that the transcendental patterns of space would be formed by the deepest psychological structures and therefore core ones to the constitutive sensibility of human experience.

We know that the very notion of country has accurate geographical, historical and cultural limits and that they are normally imposed upon the individual. This notion limits itself and controls others. On the other hand, the notion of place moves away from ideological occlusion and tends to the universal. It was not a long-time ago that Michael Jacklin (2009: 1) mentioned the "transnational dimensions of the national literature" and "the internationalizing of Australian Literature". In the case of Les Murray, as with the poets Seamus Heaney (1939-2013), Patrick Kavanagh (1904-67), José Angel Valente (1929-2000), Kakinomoto Hitomaro (died 708) and the German poets of Romanticism—paradoxical as one can apparently interpret, accounting for the ideas of Johann Gottfried von Herder (1744-1803) on nation and Volk—. But the produced dislocation is not so much the kind of typical dislodgement of the modern world as the reaching of the universal through the tangible and feasible; this is the case of place in Les Murray's poetry. A good example could be "The Body in Physics" from *Poems the Size of Photographs*

> The air has sides, in a house.
> Birds, whacked from colliding, embrace
> its sheer with umbrella-rib skiddings.
> They gape silent death-cries when closed
> in converging hands, or snatched out
> of such parts of their theory as still fly.
> Carried outside, they pause a beat
> and drop upwards, into gravity that once more
> blows as well as sucks. Fliers' gravity.

As we know one of the deepest observations of Albert Einstein over the significance of relativity is that it cancels the separation between the secular concepts of time and distance, so physicists instinctively accept that reality is described through variable space-time functions. Nevertheless, for most people, to grasp relativity they need to disassemble intuitive concepts widely settled such as time and space.

Writers of science fiction have exploited the literary possibilities of this phenomenon, but we do not exclusively have to rely upon narrative to see the possibilities, poetry also pays due to it. For us the hope is not so much what is already understood, but the mysteries yet to understand. The mysteries of this world have not been solved yet. Niels Bohr (1885-1962), one of the last century greatest physicists summarized his views on a debate on matter when talking to Wolfgang Pauli after his presentation of the Heisenberg-Pauli nonlinear generalized functions and explanations of elementary particles at Columbia University in 1958 (but upon the same terms extensible to other realms): "We are all agreed that your theory is crazy. The question that divides us is whether it is crazy enough to have a chance of being correct".

In relation to this we can see how in many poems by Les Murray we appreciate a kind of balance among relativity, universality authority and multiplicity. In many examples they are fusions of time-place and place-time, they could be understood as meditations but if they are something it is expansive place-moments or trans-time places. They belong to the process of self-perception and produce a paradox between the individuality of human perception and a universe governed by non-apprehensible complex, laws. We can see them in the poem "The Meaning of Existence"

> Everything except language
> knows the meaning of existence.
> Trees, planets, rivers, time
> know nothing else. They express it
> moment by moment as the universe.
> Even this fool of a body
> lives it in part, and would
> have full dignity within it
> but for the ignorant freedom
> of my talking mind.

Or in "Laconics: The Forty Acres"

> We have bought the Forty Acres,
> prime bush land.
> If Bunyah is a fillet
> This paddock is the eye
> The creek half-moons it,
> log-deep or parting rocks.
> The corn-ground by now
> has had forty years' grassed spell.
> Up in the swamp

are paperbarks, coin-sized frogs—
The Forty, at last,
our beautiful deep land
it was Jim's, it was Allan's,
it was Reg's, it is Dad's—
Brett wanted it next
but he'd evicted Dad:
for bitter porridge
many cold returns.
That interior machine-gun,
my chainsaw, drops dead timber.
Where we burn the heaps
we'll plant kikuyu grass.
Ecology? Sure.
But also husbandry,
and the orchard will go there,
and we'll re-roof the bare pole barn.
Our croft, our Downs,
our sober, shining land.

Bunyah in Les Murray's poetry is space humanized; it is the externalizing of experiencing consciousness. Martin Leer (2001: 16) referred to place in Murray as a 'hierophany', an "apperception of a cosmic centre", it is a place that is time, because it allows an axis for the future, and it is clearly related to Seamus Heaney's notion of *Omphalos*. Sometimes when one reads Murray's poems such as "The China Pear Trees", appearing in *The Daylight Noon* (1987) one appreciates that there is even a generative time ventured into the landscape, but it is also like a cosmic tree trespassing time and the world axis. We could even say that Seamus Heaney is directly linked to Mossbawam, as Dereck Walcott is linked to St. Lucia, as Les Murray is equally linked to Bunyah. If time and space are fused for many according to the theory of Relativity, in Murray landscape and mindscape are also merged. Bunyah place is not only his place, the place where he grew up, but also his family place, but equally a place that branches into cosmic spheres. It is worth paying attention to the fact that in an interview guided by Barbara Williams in Toronto on 23 October 1991, Les Murray referred to the idea of 'fusion' and to what he considered the distinction between a poem and a 'poeme':

> When you make a work, be it a poem, or a completed fusion such as I'm describing, it contains spiritual power and people can contemplate it and touch it, or draw energy and grace from it. There's all the difference in the world between that and an incomplete fusion, which is what I call a "poeme", which is, say, a big ideology, or somebody's own private obsession. Something like that-which contains all the elements of a poem, but isn't a final completed form, and in fact, is delaying fusion. (Williams, 1991: 48-49)

Helen Lambert (2010: 45) made a distinction between the consideration of some commentators: "critics often interpret Murray as a poet of place", but equally recognizing that "we find poems that regularly go beyond the strictures of place, and that might seem, were it not for Murray's radical transformation of the English language, to be perfectly translatable, meaningful or present". This clearly states the afore mentioned time-place merging in Murray or the 'beyondness' of place through time. Linked to this Zhang Longxi (2013: 139) reminded us how in the Chinese tradition different means of interpretations "have been more readily acknowledged than in the West and accepted with greater tolerance; relativism does not seem to be the bugbear that every critic holds in absolute abhorrence". We know that it is well-grounded in the traditional Chinese culture because even the Confucian scholars accept the arbitrary nature of language and admit the elementary plurality of meaning. This kind of thought exceeds exclusive interpretations and allows synthesis and the syncretic open-mindedness, something that suits well the pluralistic spirit of the pleasure of reading.

Another important element in Murray's poetry that has been underlined by John Kinsella (2004) is his 'organism'. In many of his poems, for example those from *Translations from the Natural World* (1992) poems like "Eagle Pair," "Insect Mating Flight," "Cockspur Bush," "The Snake's Heat Organ," "Pigs," "Spermaceti," or "Raven, Sotto Voce", the reader appreciates that the poet can bend language into marvelous constructs leading us to profound ways. He reaches that thanks to his imaginative ability to use language and moving easily within poetic constraints and conventions or making use of experimental ways. John Kinsella has stated that "there is a sense of moving through time and space, towards some metaphysical consciousness states in Murray's poetry". It is a poetry that captures the phases of human life, but also goes beyond that by registering the life cycle and some of the intricacies of nature in the universe. Murray gets away from the ancient Greek distinction between bios—the form of socially conditioned, collective and individuated life—and zoē—signifying the simple fact of living—. Murray's nature vision is close to the kind of aboriginal integrative cosmovision that Michael R. Griffiths (2013: 10) explains and where there is no distinction between bios and zoē. It is both collective and individual; it defies a "biopolitical notion of life" and has more to do with "kinship and belonging vested in country" (2013: 10). It is earthbound poetry and it is a production that looks forward to rewilding and reconnecting with land.

A good example of it is 'Cockspur Bush'

Cockspur Bush

I am lived. I am died.
I was two-leafed three times, and grazed,
but then I was stemmed and multiplied,
sharp-thorned and caned, nested and raised,
earth-salt by sun-sugar. I was innerly sung
by thrushes who need fear no eyed skin thing.
Finched, ant-run, flowered, I am given the years
in now fewer berries, now more of sling
out over directions of luscious dung.
Of water crankshaft, of gases the gears
my shape is cattle-pruned to a crown spread sprung
above the starve-gut instinct to make prairies
of everywhere. My thorns are stuck with caries
of mice and rank lizards by the butcher bird.
Inches in, baby seed-screamers get supplied.
I am lived and died in, vine woven, multiplied

This poet is a multidimensional one, the reader can travel and sense it attending to Australian nature, and in this case we can see Les Murray as the "poet of the bush", and the bush as the stretch of land covered with bushy cockspur, a species of Echinochloa crusgalli. It could be a "bush ballad" or even a celebration of his "spirit country" and a kind of poetry inspired in the physical surroundings or, as we think, something that transcends this heartland celebration and dives into the very core of nature and crushes conceptions of our human perceptions means of measuring. Helen Lambert (2010: 49) mentioned the fact that the pronouncement "shatters the unity of the speaking subject by disrupting grammatical time. The cockspur bush is simultaneously of the present and the past". It is true that the poem presents fauna and flora, it is a translation of nature, but it is also a rendering of time-place, a process that translates, that speaks in blocks and where disjoining is not possible.

Conclusion

It may be that Murray's poetry presents a poetics that has a no-place or that Bunyah is his not own place or a dislocation place, even a no-place place, a kind of metaphysical condition, a place of absolute interiority. In the case of Murray, his poetics, when it appears, when it is truly expressed, it invites us to visit this extreme territory, a territory of extreme interiority, a place of no-place, a generative space, a womb and matrix, a matter of the past projected into the future, a material future of memories and of memories of the future. For the poet place is also "where landscape and mindscape converge" (Leer 2001: 16). Place is also dynamic and the visions of nature, his visions of the world are "on the move". If place is characteristically static, place in Murray is away from conventions, it is an organic abode and a dwelling for time free. It allows backwardness and forwardness of horizons. Les Murray's place is also metamorphic and is 'aplaced' through time, it dwells through transversalities. An importance trace that verifies the statements can be found in a review that Murray himself undertook of the book *A Million Wild Acres* (1981), a book of environmental history by the Australian essayist and historian Eric C. Rolls that won The Age Book of the Year and the C.J. Dennis Prize and Talking Book of the Year. In the review, that Les Murray titled "Eric Rolls and the Golden Disobedience" the poet not only praises the book, but also identifies himself with the author's vision:

> In Rolls' presentation, things human and non-human are all happening interrelatedly, and the humans barely stand out. Through a fusion of vernacular elements with fine-grained natural observation, and a constant movement of back-reference, he breaks through sequential time not to timelessness but to a sort of enlarged spiritual present in which no life is suppressed. (1982: 48)

Nirvana Tanoukhi (2013: 306) agreed with Neil Smith's interpretation (2000: 724) of "space" as a kind of seemingly "simple, abstract category (not unlike "labor") whose conceptualization, articulation and manifestation..." is more interpreted like an "intercourse between humans and the physical universe of which they are part". In Murray, when we talk on 'space', on 'place', we refer to movable dimensions, not absolute location. It is a relative space away from a materialist definition and one that reprocesses itself mixing human and non-human elements.

On the one hand, Murray's poetry of place is a true decolonizer as it implies a reconceptualization of time-place and as it makes us change our set of perception and ethical criteria. It takes us to a new weaving of relationships between the human and non-human aggregates. It moves us to a rediscovery of existing dimensions. It is always a transboundary production taking us to the grafting or imbrication with beings and non-beings of nature. On the other hand, the conception of the universality of Murray's poetry has to do with its qualitative sense. Before Goethe proposed the notion of world literature, another German, Friedrich Schlegel (1772-1829) presented the concept of *Universalpoesie* (D'Haen 2013: 132). A. Owen Aldridge (1969: 2) explained that what he meant was a synthesis of both prose and poetry, artistic and popular, "comprising essentially everything which exists from the largest to the smallest literary system or artistic manifestation". It is just what Les Murray does.

Works Cited

Aldridge, A. Owen. *Comparative Literature: Matter and Method*. Urbana: University of Illinois Press, 1969.

——."The Universal in Literature", Theo D'Haen et al. ed., *World Literature: A Reader*. London and New York: Routledge, 2013.

Bourke, Lawrence. *A Vivid Steady State: Les Murray and Australian Poetry*. Kensington: University of New South Wales Press and New Endeavour Press, 1992.

Chaissen, Dan. "Fire Down Below: The Poetry of Les Murray", The New Yorker 11 June (2007): http://www.newyorker.com/magazine/2007/06/11/fire-down-below?printable=true

Clark, Gary. "History and Ecology. The Poetry of Les Murray and Gary Snyder", *Interdisciplinary Studies in Literature and Environment*, 10.1 Winter (2003): 27-53.

Dyson, F.J. "Innovation in Physics", *Scientific American*, 199, No. 3, September (1958): 74-82.

Elliot, Brian. *The Jindyworobaks*. Australia: University of Queensland, 1979.

Griffiths, Michael R. "Indigenous Life Writing: Rethinking Poetics and Practice", Belinda Wheeler ed., *A Companion to Australian Aboriginal Literature*. New York: Camden House, 2013.

Jaklin, Michael. "The Transnational Turn in Australian Literary Studies", *Journal of the Association for the Study of Australian Literature*, vol. Special Issue: Australian Literature in a Global World (2009): 1-14.

Kinross-Smith, Graeme. "The Frequent Image of Farms—A Profile of Les Murray", *Westerly*, Volume 25, 3, September (1980): 38-52.

Kinsella, John. "Les Murray", http://www.johnkinsella.org/essays/murray.html, 2004.

Lambert, Helen. "The Australian Language Forest: Les Murray's Translations from the Natural World", COLLOQUY text theory critique 19 (2010): 43-55.

Leer, Martin. "This Country is My Mind: Les Murray Poetics of Place", *Australian Literary Studies,* Volume 20, Number 2, October (2001): 15-42.

Longxi, Zhang. "Towards Interpretative Pluralism", Theo D'Haen et al. ed., *World Literature: A Reader*. London and New York: Routledge, 2013.

Murray, Les A. "Eric Rolls and the Golden Disobedience", *Quadrant*, Vol. 26, No. 12, Dec (1982): 44-53.

Petıfi, János S. and Terry Olivi, eds. *Approaches to Poetry: Some Aspects of Textuality, Intertextuality and Intermediality*. Berlin: De Gruyter, 1994.

Porter, Peter. "New Collected Poems by Les Murray", *The Guardian*, 15th March (2003), http://www.theguardian.com/books/2003/mar/15/featuresreviews.guardianreview13

Rolls, Eric Charles. *A Million Wild Acres: 200 Years of Man and an Australian Forest*. Melbourne: Nelson, 1981.

Smith, Neil. "Scale", Ronald J. Johnston et al. ed., 4th ed., *Dictionary of Human Geography*. London: Blackwell, 2000.

Tanoukhi, Nirvana. "The Scale of World Literature", Theo D'Haen et al. ed., *World Literature: A Reader*. London and New York: Routledge, 2013.

Williams, Barbara. "An Interview with Les A. Murray", *Westerly*, Volume 37, 2, Winter (1992): 45-56.

Wroe, Nicholas. "A Life in Writing: Les Murray", *The Guardian*, 22th November (2010), http://www.theguardian.com/books/2010/nov/22/les-murray-poet-life-profile?INTCMP=SRCH

2

Autobiographical Underpinnings in Patrick White's *The Solid Mandala*

Deepak Kumar Singh

Set largely in the fictional suburban milieu of Sarsaparilla, *The Solid Mandala* revolves around the lives and thought of Arthur and Waldo Brown. These twins become the focus of a convoluted and textured narrative that can be treated from many perspectives. *The Solid Mandala* is a challenging novel but it is rewarding to make the effort to become familiar with its nuances at first hand. *The Solid Mandala* (1966) is a story of two brothers, one cosmically inclined and 'mad', the other schizoid yet 'sane'. The book displays not only Patrick White's interest in the ideas of Jung, but his willingness to experiment with black comedy and kitchen-sink realism. One finds in this novel no synoptic vision trying to encompass expansive macrocosms. In the sense that on the surface of it, the novel does not try to hold within its narrative canvas extensive timeframes, an enormous cast of characters or an extremely convoluted widespread narrative. It is concerned with two twins and their consciousness that defines the world they live in and colors their interaction with people. *The Solid Mandala* is about two twins—Waldo and Arthur. However, in a strange and poetic journey, we realize that it can transcend the bounds of their microcosm to envelop more cosmic strains. Into the ostensibly simple tapestry of the lives of two non-descript men from the suburbs of Sydney, are woven threads linked to questions such as the nature of artistic creation, the search for spiritual and emotional wholeness, the holocaust and an impinging ethos of materialism.

Patrick White is of course Australia's most famous novelist. He lived for some time in exile but returned to Australia and lived there for some years before dying some years ago. He was a somewhat prickly character but his winning of the Nobel Prize for literature helped solidify his reputation.

This book is unusual in is clarity and sheer joy. A number of White's books are heavy going, densely written and pretentious. This book however is simply sheer delight. It concerns two old men who live together and are brothers. One is reasonably intelligent and has worked in a library. The other is what might be described as intellectually simple. The book consists of both of these characters speaking and talking about their lives and their past. White was a gay man who lived most of his life with a companion who he was deeply attached to. One suspects that the book is loosely based on their later life, but of course this is only speculation. The character who is most hardly done by is the librarian who clearly is White.

The narrative is divided into four unequal parts. Brief opening and closing sections have Mrs. Poulter as the principle actor. According to Thelma Herring, these sections "form a frame which puts the timeless theme in a contemporary context" (Herring, 73). The expository section introduces the bachelor twins through the perspectives of Mrs. Poulter and Mrs. Dun as revealed in a conversation that they have as they ride the bus between Sarsaparilla and Barranugli. The exterior sections impose the outside world's perspectives on the narrative even as it subtly critiques that world's materialistic values and narrowness of vision. The two central parts recount the lives and thoughts of Waldo and Arthur from Waldo's perspective first and then more briefly from Arthur's perspective. These sections deal more extensively with two seemingly antithetical approaches to life in that society, which through the device of the twins, are shown to be also almost inextricably linked.

The narrative takes off with a bus journey in which Mrs. Poulter and Mrs. Dun are introduced directly and the Brown brothers obliquely through their conversation. In this section called 'In the Bus', the Brown brothers are shown stumbling along the road between Barranugli and Sarsaparilla with their blue terriers, Runt and Scruffy. There is a combination of the omniscient narrator commenting on the thoughts and nature of the two women, the women being characterized through their overt actions and words, as well as women indirectly characterizing the Browns through their observations.

The narrator hints repetitively at the narrow and materialistic perspectives Mrs. Dun and Mrs. Poulter are able to bring to bear on the things they talk about. For example, when Mrs. Poulter comments that some women end up spending a shilling in order to save the occasional half-penny, the narrator reveals to us how Mrs. Dun mentally fixates on this piece of information. Having made the appropriate calculations for the half-penny, she is fascinated that some women may actually be losing one-and-eleven on a shopping trip between Sarsaparilla and Barranugli. The significance of these minute details in their lives is underscored time and again, throughout this first section. Mrs. Poulter and Mrs. Dun had met for the first time only recently on a similar bus ride, in spite of them both having lived on the same road for years. As they discuss what brought them both to Terminus Road, Mrs. Poulter mentions her neighbors, the Mister Browns. Mrs. Dun is simultaneously put off by the possibility that the Browns may be her social superiors and pacified by the fact that they are from England. The pettiness of her focus is evinced when she picks out for negative comment things like the strangeness of Waldo's name and the fact that the two aged brothers are holding each other's hands. The former is to her indicative of snobbish elitism and the latter of the possible perversity of the two men. Her observations reveal her insecurities and the limited nature of her mental horizons. This section also presents through these two women the socio-cultural frame within which the story of Waldo and Arthur unfolds.

The Brown brothers are concretized by these two ladies as at once repulsive but intriguing, almost hideous and pitiable to the outsider or onlooker. On Mrs. Dun the impression is totally negative. She 'resentfully' notices the two old men, stumping, 'trudging' almost 'tottering' along worn down by their 'age and infirmities' and 'holding each other by the hand' (18-19). The sense of repulsion she feels, but cannot quite quantify, has been echoed earlier in Mr. Poulter's contemptuous dismissal of them as a 'couple of no-hopers with ideas about themselves' (18). Their only demotically, Mrs. Poulter, too finds her unable to go on defending them and disowns them reiterating Mrs. Dun's 'They're nothing to me' (19). The exposition sets the dismal tone for a narrative which reveals, as William Walsh puts it, that the two brothers, "are handcuffed, as they grope down the path negotiating the irregular bricks, by love and hate, memory and genes, horror and misery" (Walsh, 86).

The second and third sections, named 'Waldo' and 'Arthur' respectively tell the same story through two perspectives. Here again the characterization is through a combination of the omniscient narrator commenting mostly on the brother used to focalize the text, direct characterization of the brother concerned through his thoughts and actions and his indirect characterization of the other players in the drama of his life. As in the other sections, even when the author privileges a particular point of view by giving it almost complete say in 'telling' the story, he also uses the omniscient narrator to balance that point of view by revealing its own biases.

Relationships form the thematic content of the two intermediate sections. Thelma Herring points out that one can read the predominant emotion dominating the 'Waldo' section as hatred born of deep seated insecurity and increasing isolation (Herring, 75). Waldo has a deep sense of being chained in a disadvantageous relationship to his twin brother. As a result of this, he either has to suffer being excluded when Arthur is patronizingly preferred over him because of his disability or the equally strong sense of mortification of constantly being associated with Arthur. His greatest sense of humiliation and anger however, is to see Arthur actually doing and surpassing him in the areas he deems his territory. Thus, that Arthur manages to capture and hold Dulcie's affection, that Arthur reads literary classics and is disturbed by the larger questions of life they raise and that Arthur actually writes, are blows that quite devastate

Waldo's construction of a superior self-image in relation to his brother. The loss of this image, both gradually throughout his life and more suddenly towards the close of his narrative infuse his being with palpable abhorrence for things and people, springing from personal despair as the success and place in life he had envisaged for himself slip further out of his reach.

If hatred for others and an incipient self-hatred are part of Waldo's constitution of himself, then the third section devoted to and entitled 'Arthur' is infused with the thematic concerns of positive relationships and an almost religious spiritual search for wholeness. Most of the episodes that figure in the Waldo section are reining scribed here through the mellow perspective of Arthur. What were sources of humiliation for Waldo, become sources of affection and part of a continued process of personal enlightenment for Arthur?

Although they are twins, and although "the lives of the brothers fused by consent at some points" (81), they are opposites, physically, mentally and spiritually points out Thelma Herring. Waldo is depicted as a pseudo-intellectual, who excels at writing English essays and becomes a librarian. He assumes a sense of superiority that fuels and legitimizes his hatred of and scorn for the people around him. Waldo, however, has aspirations to be a novelist when he eventually hopes to find something to write about. The elitist and esoteric view of art and himself, he holds fails to keep him in touch with the realities that could have nourished his aspirations into fruition. Arthur is portrayed as an alleged simpleton, who is a failure at school except for a surprising flair for figures, becomes a grocer's assistant and humbly accepts the realities around him. He loves and is loved by people (and dogs) and seeks to share a redemptive totality with the lives of those he touches. "Their experiences, however often coincide: they love the same woman (after their different fashions), both write "poems" and read books, each acquires a dog, both on occasion play the woman, both give Mrs. Poulter a "child" (Waldo in the form of a plastic doll, Arthur by accepting the relationship himself), each is accosted by a whore on the night that the Second World War ends, each becomes in a sense the other's murderer." To Mrs. Dun, watching from the bus as they walk hand in hand, "It was difficult to decide which was leading and which was being led. But one was the leader, she could sense" (19). Waldo, of course, believes himself to be the leader, and the protector of Arthur; Arthur feels from the beginning that he is protected, and is the protector of his whole family (Herring, 73-74). The denouement reveals that both visions of life though seemingly at odds with one another interpenetrate one another, constituting parts of a whole.

The final section, like the opening section, imposes the perspective of the outside world onto the narrative. As in the opening section, the closing section entitled, 'Mrs. Poulter and the Zeitgeist' combines negative impressions of the fate of the Brown brothers and a more positive apprehension of the same by Mrs. Poulter. Only this time her perspective holds sway over the denouement giving it a stronger sense of thematic coherence.

To touch upon some more autobiographical and personal notes that impinges upon the book: "White testifies in Flaws in the Glass to his own anxiety at the time he was writing *The Solid Mandala*. He and his friend Lascaris had decided to move from "Dog woods," their home of many years, because the suburban nuisances were becoming oppressive. He feared that the uprooting might be fatal to his writing, that *The Solid Mandala* might be his "swan song". Inevitably the novel "was infused with an amount of fatality and foreboding." For those interested in the sources of White's inspiration and possible prototypes of his characters, he identifies the twins as "my two halves," with Waldo as "myself at my coldest and worst." Mrs. Poulter "grew out of a neighbor lady", and Dulcie "has both the goodness and the smugness of a fulfilled Jewish acquaintance" (Jones, 72-73).

The Solid Mandala, is densely overlaid with thematic interpretations and readings of the narrative. Most of these themes are textually worked out through the twins, Waldo and Arthur. As a result, much overlapping of thematic possibilities takes place. As a framework to explore the possibilities this novel lays open, several of the thematic preoccupations of this novel have been listed. It is for us to add to or take away from this list as your own reading breathes life into this thematic skeleton and fills it out with the flesh and, blood of the character's actions and thoughts.

Waldo and Arthur embody an almost Nietzschean theme of the lonely agnostic's agonized quest for the capacity of insight into the very nature of things. Waldo's futile struggle to exert his sense of identity leads him further and further along the path of alienated isolation. Arthur takes up the pursuit of meaning against the enervating rationalism of his family and reaches for a greater understanding of mankind, the nature of existence, pain and totality. He manifests a longing for truths beyond material knowledge—the nature of redemption, the large meaning and design of life. The semi-mystical vortex of the narrative climaxes at a final epiphany that leaves them both tormented by their vision and humanity.

The Solid Mandala is suffused with a confluence of religious motifs drawn from across the spectrum of Oriental tantric mandalas to Occidental allusions to Judeo-Christianity. This theme of religious responsibility is played out in the relationship between the two brothers:

> White works out an intimate connection of transcendental and rationalistic attitudes in the twins Arthur and Waldo. The intimacy and inescapability of the relationship between them produces a constant and destructive collision of viewpoints, and confronts Arthur again and again with his responsibility toward a temperament hostile to the values his mysticism has led him to cherish. He cannot voluntarily renounce his brother...because he has not voluntarily taken him on. And it is from this agonizing, tense contiguity of opposites that the book derives part of its disturbing power. (Edgecombe, 62)

This theme manifests itself variously—as Waldo's sense of failure as a writer, his failure to win Dulcie—quotidian and worldly failure. To this Carolyn Bliss adds, "The failure of love to be strong enough to save is a familiar vehicle for the theme of failure in Patrick White's fiction" (Bliss, 110). Arthur feels this sense of failure when he finds his love fails to integrate Waldo fully into the mandalic dance, to negate the consuming power of Waldo's hatred—spiritual and cosmic failure. White's preoccupation with failure as a theme draws on his belief that, "The mystery of life is not solved by success, which is an end in itself, but in failure, in perpetual struggle, in becoming" (Joyce, 47).

The imaginary suburbs of Sarsaparilla in the *The Solid Mandala*, acquire the status of the fictional landscape of Faulkner's Yoknapatawpha, Joyce's Dublin, Hardy's Wessex or Arundhati Roy's Ayemenem. The role of the everyday folk in Sarsaparilla, like Mr. Poulter or Mrs. Dun, is to represent the dull, commonplace, ignorant averageness that made for:

> 'the Great Australian Emptiness' as White saw it. Sarsaparilla inscapes or captures the sterility and materialism of White's vision of a spiritual wasteland. According to Ken Goodwin, the place is modeled on the Castle Hill suburb, which used to be the home of White and Lascaris before they moved to the heart of the city. (Goodwin, 169)

When the narrative opens it is in a "a place once a village now a suburb, in which the remnants of the country die in the suburban landscape" (Walsh, 85). In this mildly caustic idyll of suburban life, Australia is center stage. The larger world impinges in the form of the Jewish question and the allusions to the World War and the holocaust. But these are worked into the lives of the Brown brothers in such a way as to condense the macrocosmic upheavals—such as the holocaust or the Peace—into the microcosms of their personal failures, tragedies of rejection or acceptance. The narrative keeps them within the perspective of the lives of the twins. The Jewish question becomes coalesced with attempts to establish a relationship with Dulcie Feinstein, and the end of the Second World War is marked for both brothers by encounters with prostitutes. According to Walsh, White evokes:

> not only the exact registration of the physical appearance of the place, but also a sense of the community's reaction, its ethos and feeling. There is a considerable stress on the rougher and more abrasive elements of Australian common life. The names of the people and places, for example, are

> redolent of a kind of truculent glumness: Wally Pugh, Mrs. Purves, Mrs. Musto, Mrs. Mutton, Norm Croucher, the dogs Scruffy and Runt, O'Halloran Road, Ada Avenue, Sarsaparilla, Barranugli, Shadbolt Lane, GippaGunyan, Mungindribble. The ugliness these names stand for is confirmed by the half aggressive idiom which is the common idiom of communication and the two together convey, negatively and positively, the feeling of a society which is both traditionally and visually uneducated, and possessed of an openness and freedom untrammeled by the weight of an oppressive inheritance. (Walsh, 88)

As Mr. Brown said once to Waldo and Arthur, "There's too much you boys, reared in the light of an empty country, will never understand. There aren't any shadows in Australia. Or discipline. Every man jack can do what he likes" (161).

Sarsaparilla is debunked in the final section when the modern idea of comfort and material progress in the suburbs is reduced to "the electricity...the phone...the electric frying-pan... the telly" (295). It's a closed world, where human relationships become just habits and the television is a substitute for friends. Mrs. Poulter muses:

> If she didn't have any friends without the ones she yarned with over fences, in buses, or the street, she didn't need any. She had the telly, the nice announcers, and world figures in your own lounge. She could afford to mind her own business, without Mrs. Dun reminding her of it. (295)

The outer socio-political reality barely impinges on this microcosm of self-complacent containment. The real world is transformed into a hyperreal source of diversion from moments of unpleasantness in local life—for example when Mrs. Poulter's pigs are butchered. Mrs. Poulter waited most for "the real programmes, when they let off one of the bombs, or an aeroplane caught fire at the moment of crashing, or those guerillas they'd collared, of course they were only Orientals, and once it showed you the bodies they'd shot...the news items so real, you only sometimes overheard the squeals of a stuck and bleeding pig" (299).

Only after she sees the dead and mutilated Waldo, at the end of the narrative, do these become realities she can connect with; even if in her imagination they metamorphosize into a kind of armageddon:

> She knew now. All the films, all the telly, all the black-and-white of the papers was turning real, as the great clouds, the great tanks, ground up groaning over Sarsaparilla.... Hope was faint. She knew now. The flat faces of all those Chinese guerillas or Indonesians, it was the same thing, dragged out across the dreadful screen. All those Jews in ovens, that was long ago, but still burning, lying in heaps. Lone women bashed up in Mosman, Marouba, Randwick, places you went only in your sleep. (302)

Veena Noble suggests that "Perhaps the most common theme of Australian literature is the lack of intensity, passion and spiritual consciousness in middle-class life" (Noble, 31). However, this is a theme that has begun to wear thin and sit uneasily with an Australian audience. Adrian Mitchell traces this phenomenon with reference to:

> that collective state of mind or mindlessness, called Sarsaparilla. When White first began writing of this social territory, his readers shared his savage delight as he slashed his way through the values, the speech patterns, the affectations of mid-suburban Australia. The consensus is that he was wickedly accurate. He had the mannerisms down... and he knew just how to expose the private vulgarities. The public vulgarities were easy game.... He had discovered the subtleties of the demotic, he knew the vulnerable spots... he understood the true function of gossip in a social group, the definitions that small talk established.... Sarsaparilla has become a convention. (Mitchell, 14-15)

While admitting that White's work has put Australian literature on the world map, Kirpal Singh says that he would not add:

> that White's work gives us the Australian character or, indeed, is even a representative of Australian society! Even Sarsaparilla which appears to be firmly located as some

> recognizably Australian suburb could just as well have been situated in any of the big European cities. Subtle nuances and cadences aside, there is nothing particularly Australian in an ethos whose chief characteristics are a vulgarity of living and an emptiness of sour. (Singh, 119)

The narrative manner of this novel is, as in all White's major work, "thick with explicit particulars. Everything is embodied and illustrated. Each shade of feeling or quirk of action is solidly realized.... The narrative technique...swoops and turns and flicks from point to point, with a logic different from simple sequence," comments William Walsh. He goes on to draw comparisons between White's narrative technique and D.H. Lawrence's formulations on "the movement of the emotional mind" which speaks of how "...the mind makes curious swoops and circles. It touches the point of pain or interest, then swoops and circles, coils round and approaches again the point of pain or interest...." In the text, for example, the frame narrative for the 'Waldo' section is constituted by a walk the brothers take on Waldo's suggestion.... The same walk during which Mrs. Dun and Mrs. Poulter had seen them in the opening section. Arthur proposes that if they hang around they might meet Mrs. Poulter and walk together to the bus. Waldo refuses the suggestion but the reference to Mrs. Poulter sets off a train of reminisces that go back to his childhood memories. The narrative from there moves back and forth between the walk and snatches from the past—for Waldo, mostly memories tinged with pain and humiliation. Walsh continues:

> In *The Solid Mandala* the procedure is one of shading and emphasis, of varying the point of entrance and sweeping backwards and forwards in a way which impresses the reader as a composition rather than a linear progress. (Walsh, 86-87)

Walsh's observations apply more to the 'Waldo' section which constitutes the bulk of the text than to the 'Arthur' section which is more linear in its narrative progression. In fact, Arthur's narrative opens with an "In the beginning there was the sea..." (215) with its Biblical intonations echoing the opening words of the book of Genesis. Carolyn Bliss too discusses

White's technique of producing an "evocative blending of a novel's themes and motifs in a single scene, a practice which seems to owe as much to music as to literature." She cites one of the best examples for this as coming "from *The Solid Mandala*, for, in Arthur's mandalic dance, imagistic motifs associated with each major character and with several thematic concerns are counterpointed in a comprehensive pattern which centers the novel's meaning in a possible order, harmony and wholeness" (Bliss, 198-99).

To bring out the hieratic nature of Arthur's apprehension of reality, White infuses the narrative with religious allusions, quasi-sacramental motifs and a heightened sense of poetry. This is however juxtaposed with the demotic nature of the icons through which this apprehension of reality is purveyed. The demotic and hieratic, the mundane and the elevated are shown to be part of one whole.

White's style and content bespoke a new voice in the Australian canon. It was both ironical and whimsical; not to mention almost surrealist in the 'Arthur' section. The novel, *The Solid Mandala*, is a minor epic about common life infused with the mystical lyricism and pulsating prose poetry of the 'Arthur' section. The thick texture in the idiom is evocative of character and social ambience in the narrative framework. William Walsh discusses White's use of language in the context of the rest of his oeuvre:

> To go from Riders in the Chariot to *The Solid Mandala* (1966), is to move from a novel which is spacious and inclusive to one in which the field of action is confined, in which the language is more abstinent, the metaphorical habit less florid, the manner altogether trimmer and sharper.... This spare novel—spare by Patrick White's standards, that is—is one of the most beautifully organized of White's works and one marked by an unusual blend of inwardness and control, life and impersonality. (Walsh, 85)

Thelma Herring warns against seeing the recurrent mordant imagery of the 'Waldo' section as all pervasive as "in Arthur's part the prose is free of it but is rich in images of religious associations" (Herring, 74). She notes however, that:

> Traversing most of the twins' life-span of seventy-years, from the time when their parents bring them from England as small children, the story is from one point of view a chronicle of senescence and decay. Both parents die, the weather board house that George Brown has built for himself on arrival begins to disintegrate, the young quince trees become wormy and woody, the sea of grass encroaches more and more, the young dogs, like the brothers themselves, grow old and feeble: in Waldo's part, startling images of squalor and decay (mice nesting in burst leather chair, mutton fat curdling in skeins, and so on enforce the impression of lives petering out in sterile loneliness (but also reflect the mental obliquity of Waldo). (Herring, 74)

This is shown to be a matter of Waldo's perspective and the point of view he brings to bear on life. The images are indicative of Waldo's spiritual decay and enervation.

McCulloch commenting on the sensuous imagery used in association with Arthur says, "Arthur seems to be the essence of the senses themselves. White communicates this by descriptions of Arthur which are markedly different in texture from those reserved for Waldo." Arthur is able to hear and "see in advance the splotches of sound" (232); he "would roll on his seat in time with the buggy long before its motion called for it" (234); can "smell the smell of cold mud" (246) and "sing shapeless songs" (251). "The language used for the 'Arthur section' succeeds in interrelating the senses when touching the world" (McCulloch, 34). As in the case of Waldo, these images reflect Arthur's character and the way in which he frames reality.

Moving to a more general apprehension of how the book uses figurative language, Carolyn Bliss offers an interesting intervention on the subject. "White sometimes fashions a continuum of imagery, from the ant on the pavement to the sun in the sky, which sets man as a middle term and suggests that all share the same vital impulse. Alternately, actions may illuminate each other by their contiguity. For example, in The Solid Mandala, Mrs. Feinstein tells Arthur and Waldo about visiting her European relatives:

> I don't know what Daddy would have to say to so much Jewish emotionalism. I was thankful we did not have him with us, either in Paris or Milan. 'Poor things, they are devout.' Mrs. Feinstein smiled for the sick, though it could have been she enjoyed the illness. 'Of course we did whatever was expected of us while we were there. We did not have the heart to tell them we have given up all such middle-aged ideas, to conform,' she said, 'to conform with the spirit of progress. Daddy, I am afraid, who is more forceful in his expression, would have offended.' After that she disappeared, trailing the outdoor coat she was wearing. It was so out of place. It was so shapeless it might have been inherited. (132)

Simply by appending the trailed, 'inherited' coat to Mrs. Feinstein's smugly modern point of view, White comments ironically on her hope that the inheritance of faith may be discarded. At the same time, "the repetition of the word 'conform' suggests that her modernism reflects nothing more than capitulation to a new kind of pressure" (Bliss, 198). Such subtle use of imagery infuses the text with nuances that can be picked up only with multiple and careful reading, as well as creative interpretation. As in the case of Arthur's marbles, it involves seeing the possibilities of the putatively mundane.

Patrick White's avowed desire to rise above realistic writing and discover the poetry and mystery encapsulated in ordinary lives has made him extensively use mythopoeic elements in his works. His works embody a structure or framework linked to myths and parallel motifs. *The Solid Mandala* is no exception, though how exactly he has employed these elements and to what effect remains a matter of interpretation. He has drawn on Christian motifs, beginning with the Adam and Eve motif in The Tree of Man right through to the crucifixion motif in Riders in the Chariot. Marshall Best sees a continuation of this trend in his interpretation of the relationship of the two brothers.

> In *The Solid Mandala*, still absorbed with aspects of the problem of personal identity, he tried out his own version of the Cain and Abel legend in a story of two contemporary brothers. (Best, 692)

Patricia Morely interprets that same relationship as allegory.

> On the allegorical level there is the further connotation of the mystery of the relationship between man's body and soul, identified with Arthur and self-will, identified with Waldo. (Morley, 5)

Equally significant is White's ability to invest an ambience of myth and cosmic symbolism replete with allusions to many kinds of religions—ancient, modern, Eastern, Western around the most mundane of situations. Life itself becomes a series of epiphanic moments for Arthur. For example, when Arthur delivers groceries, Mrs. Feinstein offers him lemonade and asks him, etc. "drink it slowly and concentrate" so he can "extract the *prana* from this lemonade" (241). Some of this is again a matter of interpretation and having an eye for details. For example, Walsh says, "The bus journey has in it a certain ritual quality, as though the two ladies were not only beating the bounds of the terrain of the novel but defining its sensibility" (Walsh, 85). Similarly, Thelma Herring comments,

> The symbolic use of physical characteristics is in fact a marked feature of the novel. Arthur's brown eyes link him not only with his gentle father but also with Dulcie, Len Saporta, and their children...while Waldo with his "inherited eyes", pale and cold, is linked with the mother whose aristocratic connections fascinate him, and feels an affinity with other blue-eyed people. (Herring, 79)

In dealing with the serious themes he has in hand Patrick White lapses into the humorous mode very subtly and across a wide range, if at all. There is the social satire of the portrayal of the petty materialism and shallow perspectives of ordinary Sarsaparillites like Mrs. Dun. There is the homely humour of the lesser local characters like the eccentric Mrs. Musto or the snobbish Miss Dallimores when they come to tea with the Browns. There is the element of social comedy in the awkward visits of the brothers to the Feinsteins with Waldo desperately trying to maintain a façade of pseudo-respectability and Arthur's childish candour spoiling the intended effect. There is the confluence of rhetoric and mantric utterance, as in the lemonade—*prana* episode when Mrs. Feinstein just afterwards adds the rationalist caveat "Of course we don't know exactly if this is a practice which has been scientifically approved of, but it's a nice idea, don't you think?" The dark, almost pathetic comedy of Mr. Brown inadequately trying to tell Waldo about the facts of life and ending up telling him about precautions he should take with public lavatories.

Andrew Riemer puckishly points out that the religious intensity of Arthur is at times played out against a backdrop of suburban satire.

> White spoke with many voices. What has been difficult for some to recognize is that strain of mordant comedy that accompanies many of his metaphysical peaks, enriching rather than diminishing the intensity of those moments. When Arthur Brown's concentration on the mystery of things in The Solid Mandala is momentarily diverted by a falling dog, the indecent and the indecorum somehow allows us to accept the validity of this outrageous fable, an account of the quest for salvation in the pedestrian outer suburbs of Sydney. (Joyce, 158-59)

White, in the novel, employs a patois of voices and narrative points of view. The range extends from omniscient focalization, where the narrator can focalize the point of view of any character, to narration through internal point of view, presented in terms of the feelings and perceptions of characters. So most of the time, the voices are of intradiegetic narrators like Waldo, Arthur and Mrs. Dun who are personally involved in the action being narrated. This is laced with the barely distinguishable extradiegetic omniscient narrator with no involvement in the action but comments on it from the outside. The interpenetration of both points of view acts to establish balance in the composite narrative point of view. It reveals that there are ever so many stories or perspectives that emerge from an ostensibly simple single story.

Carolyn Bliss notes how shifting modes of focalization bring about shifts in our perspectives as well.

> The opening section, 'In the Bus', consists of nervous small talk which Mrs. Poulter makes while riding the bus with her

> new friend Mrs. Dun. We approach the Brown brothers as these women do, at the distance of gossip and by way of a quick glimpse from a bus window. Even the excruciatingly painful and personal events of the final section come to us filtered through the responses of others: horror and nausea of the police sergeant and his young assistant, the terror of Mrs. Dun, the ribaldry of the drunks in the alley, and the unfeeling officiousness of the librarians.... In both outer sections, the reader is kept at a certain remove. (Bliss, 101-02)

For the inner sections, Caroline Bliss notes, he uses "indirect discourse, in which the narrator's voice speaks in phrases and cadences which would be used by the character, thereby disclosing feelings, values and reactions...one of White's favorite methods for maintaining an ironic perspective on character and one of the sharpest weapons in his satiric and comedic arsenal" (Bliss, 102). There are constant shifts between authorial endorsed narrative and indirect discourse. Bliss argues that the use of indirect discourse is strategic for there is no other way to penetrate Waldo's reserve and Arthur's ramblings.

> Because Arthur is born to his visionary status, he is subjected to very little of the irony White trains on his protagonists. Waldo, on the other hand, is treated with satire more biting and contempt more unmitigated than any previous protagonist has undergone. (Bliss, 114)

White also reproduces the speech and thought of characters, using the colloquial idiom. The novelist's cool ironic mocking voice is heard in comments like "The girl Dulcie was probably poor. In her pink, as opposed to white, dress. Not that he doesn't despise Dulcie as well. In his crusade of bitterness there was only room for one ardent pauper" (89) or "Nobody remembered her husband, or knew whether she had ordered him out of existence so that she might enjoy a breezy widowhood" (85). White never attaches himself to the flow and pulse of his character's lives as a result of which he seems to mime their thinking at times making his explicit commentary seem even more supercilious and lacking in magnanimity especially in the case of Waldo.

In the novel, White lends Waldo his caustic wit to make judgments that characterize Waldo's vindictive malice more than the person on whom the judgment is passed. As when Waldo finally realizes he has lost out on Dulcie and envisions her as Saporta's wife:

> He did look back just once at Mrs. Saporta, increasing, bulging, the Goddess of a Thousand Breasts, standing at the top of her stairs, in a cluster of unborn ovoid children. This giant incubator hoped she was her own infallible investment. But she would not suck him in. Imagining to hatch him out.... So much for Dulcie Feinstein Saporta and her lust for possession. (157)

Adrian Mitchell says that these shifts in narrative focus can be read as having a rather postmodernist effect of undermining the 'truth' claim of any one perspective. "Ambiguously, the story is the set of events, at yet another level the story is only a record of the set of events, an interpretation. Hence White's fondness for alternative versions or accounts of central events—most obviously in *The Solid Mandala*" (Mitchell, 13). This perspective brings into play a combination of voices and points of view allowing the reader to make his or her own assessments.

Carolyn Bliss offers an in-depth analysis of the deployment of the time factor in *The Solid Mandala*. "The 'Waldo' section is told largely as a series of flashbacks stimulated by incidents that occur while the elderly brothers take their daily constitutional. This walk, which occupies nearly two thirds of the book, takes place probably only a few days or weeks before the murder attempt, with which the 'Waldo' section culminates. Where the 'Waldo' section was disjointed, its events standing isolated and discrete, 'Arthur' is cohesively chronological. Even in the case of the occasional brief flashback, the relationship of events to time and to each other is preserved" (Bliss, 106). She continues, "Structurally, the novels tend towards episode and epiphany.... The episodic progress of plot, interrupted by frequent and sometimes unexplained gaps in time, suggests a world in which human actions are rarely attuned to nature's rhythmic constancy...his tendency to disrupt chronology (as in *Riders in the Chariot, The Solid Mandala* and *A Fringe of Leaves*)...support a view of human experience as discontinuous and fragmentary" (Bliss, 197).

Works Cited

Ashcroft, W.D. "More Than One Horizon" in *Patrick White: A Critical Symposium*. Edited by R.E. Shepherd and Kripal Singh. Adelaide: Flinders University Centre for Research in the New Literatures in English, 1978. 123-34.

Best, Marshall A. "White Patrick (Victor Martindale)" in *Contemporary Novelists*. Edited by James Vinson. 3rd Edition. Surrey: Macmillan, 1982. 691-92.

Bliss, Carolyn. *Patrick White's Fiction: The Paradox of Fortunate Failure*. London: Macmillan, 1986.

Goodwin, Ken, *A History of Australian Literature*. London: Macmillan, 1986.

Herring, Thelma. "Self and Shadow: The Quest for totality in *The Solid Mandala*" in *Ten Essays on Patrick White Selected from Southerly* (1964-1967). Edited by G.A. Wilkes. Sydney and London: Angus and Robertson, 1970. 72-82.

Joyce, Clayton ed. *Patrick White: A Tribute*. North Ryde: Angus and Robertson, 1991.

McCulloch, A.M. *A Tragic Vision: The Novels of Patrick White*. St. Lucia: University of Queensland Press, 1983.

Mitchell, Adrian. "Eventually, White's Language: Words and More than Words" in *Patrick White: A Critical Symposium*. Edited by R.E. Shepherd and Kripal Singh. Adelaide: Flinders University Centre for Research in the New Literatures in English, 1978. 5-16.

Morley, Patricia. *Mystery of Unity: Theme and Technique in the Novels of Patrick White*. St. Lucia: University of Queensland Press, 1972.

Walsh, William. *Patrick White's Fiction*. Sydney: George Allen and Unwin, 1977.

White, Patrick. *The Solid Mandala*. London: Penguin, 1969.

3

Seeking an Answer for the Honour of the Fallen: Ada Cambridge's Feminist Issues

Sudhir K. Arora

Ada Cambridge (1844-1926), an English-born Australian poet broke the myth of inadequacy of Australian women authors at the time when there was the dominance of the male authors. The patriarchal context eclipsed and brought darkness to the women writers. But, Ada Cambridge reversed the flow of the water and set a new orientation to the forthcoming women writers. *Encyclopaedia of Post-Colonial Literatures in English* refers Cambridge's life as "crowded with duties as a mother and clergyman's wife, cruelly marked by tragedy, hampered by financial worries and confined by ill health. Yet she was a natural and thoroughly professional writer, who maintained both independence and immense popularity" (177).

Ada Cambridge does not hesitate to offer sharp criticism of her own class. She has given a force to her women to come out from the whirl of the male domination. She portrays well the humiliations and pains suffered by the Australian women from the fetters of the masculine domination. Her second poetry collection *Unspoken Thoughts* (1887) demonstrates her skill in handling the feminist issues concerning the liberation from the bondage under the male chauvinism. Honour is the word that counts for her in life. She attempts to seek an answer for the cause of the female exploitation at the hands of male members. She interrogates the established rules and conventions and offers her unconventional opinions in the age of orthodoxy and male monopolization.

Here are quoted Ada Cambridge's four poems from her poetry collections *Unspoken Thoughts*. She raises some feminist issues which were quite new and revolutionary in nature in the nineteenth century.

ONE: Honour

ME let the world disparage and despise—
This virtuous world that loves its gilded chains,
Its mean successes and its sordid gains,
Its pleasant vice and profitable lies;
Let its strong hand my rebel deeds chastise,
The rebel blood that surges in my veins,
And deal me all due penalties and pains,
And make me hideous in my neighbours' eyes.
But let me fall not in mine own esteem,
My poor deceit or selfish greed debased.
Let me be clean from secret stain and shame,
Know myself true, though only false I seem—
Know myself worthy, howsoe'er disgraced—
Know myself right, though all the world should blame. (23)

TWO: Seeking

BRIGHT eyes, sweet lips, with sudden fevers fill
My strong blood, running wildly, as it must;
But lips and eyes too soon beget distrust.
A soft touch sends a momentary thrill
Through sense unsubservient to the will;
But warm caresses leave a dim disgust;
Like Dead-Sea apples, kisses turn to dust.
I kiss; I feast; but I am hungry still.
O, where is She—that straight and upright soul—
True friend, true mate, true woman—where is She?
True heart—as true as needle to the pole—
True to the truth, not only true to me—

Worth all I have to give—the best—the whole.
When shall these eyes Her unknown beauty see? (85)
THIRD: Fallen
FOR want of bread to eat and clothes to wear—
Because work failed and streets were deep in snow,
And this meant food and fire—she fell so low,
Sinning for dear life's sake, in sheer despair.
Or, because life was else so bald and bare,
The natural woman in her craved to know
The warmth of passion—as pale buds to blow
And feel the noonday sun and fertile air.
And who condemns? She who, for vulgar gain
And in cold blood, and not for love or need,
Has sold her body to more vile disgrace—
The prosperous matron, with her comely face—
Wife by the law, but prostitute in deed,
In whose gross wedlock womanhood is slain. (56)
FOURTH: An Answer
THY love I am. Thy wife I cannot be,
To wear the yoke of servitude—to take
Strange, unknown fetters that I cannot break
On soul and flesh that should be mine, and free.
Better the woman's old disgrace for me
Than this old sin—this deep and dire mistake;
Better for truth and honour and thy sake—
For the pure faith I give and take from thee.
I know thy love, and love thee all I can—
I fain would love thee only till I die;
But I may some day love a better man,
And thou may'st find a fitter mate than I;
Some want, some chill, may steal 'twixt heart and heart.
And then we must be free to kiss and part. (87)

The poems, namely 'Honour', 'Seeking', 'Fallen', and 'An Answer' clearly reveal the freedom loving spirit of Ada Cambridge who never wishes to confine her Self at one place or in a cage of married life or domestic life. She does not care for the world—the so-called virtuous world that loves the chains—"gilded chains" which bind a free spirit and fetter its free flight in the sky of possibilities and potentialities. This world has its own successes and gains but she calls them mean and sordid respectively. Its vices may be pleasant and lies profitable. But, she avoids lies and vices howsoever they may appear pleasant or profitable. She does not care if the so-called virtuous world punishes her with its strong hand but she will continue to rebel against it. The blood of rebellion that flows in her veins cannot be suppressed or hindered in its flow despite the penalties and pains, which she is ready to bear for the sake of her honour—the honour that does not allow her to remain in the gilded chains. She does not even care for the false allegation of this gilded world that intends to prove her "hideous" in her neighbour's eye and the people as well.

The poet in Ada Cambridge believes that it is better to be true to one's self than to be true to the world. If one is true to one's Self, one cannot be wrong to the world. On the contrary, if one is wrong or deceitful to one's Self, one cannot be true to the world howsoever he may attempt to prove one's Self right from the various angles. She may fall in the estimation of the people but never wishes to fall in her own estimation of her Self.

> But let me fall not in mine own esteem,
> My poor deceit or selfish greed debased.
> Let me be clean from secret stain and shame,
> Know myself true, though only false I seem—
> Know myself worthy, howsoe'er disgraced—
> Know myself right, though all the world should blame. (23)

What counts for her is honour and her Self. She can deceive all but never her 'Self' and 'Honour'. She raises many feminist issues in her poetry, particularly in her poetry collection *Unspoken Thoughts*. It is shocking that in this male monopolized society a woman is merely an object—the object meant for the satisfaction of lust and exploitation. She is not considered to be a subject. Body dominates over her Soul. It is also strange that women do not understand the politics of the male world and so fall in the snares of being objects for the male gaze. She is crushed in bed and used badly for commercial purposes. The body becomes the object for earning dollars. She is not born weak but is made weak and the male world takes the credit of having the male's burden for her sustenance. No doubt, she becomes a beauty in the eyes of the male world for her bright eyes and sweet lips. But, these eyes and lips are of no permanent value as they bring distrust. A soft touch stirs the strings of the body which begins to feel the thrill through the sensations. But this sensation comes to an end with the end of the warm caresses which "leave a dim disgust" while disappearing like "dead-sea apples". She herself feels that she kisses and also enjoys feast but even then she remains hungry. Body feels relaxed but soul becomes restless. Where is she—the real woman? This body is not woman. This body is the form of the real woman. The physical union fails to touch the very spirit of the woman who remains restless. Mark the lines for this restlessness which she feels even after the physical relationship:

> I kiss; I feast; but I am hungry still.
> O, where is She—that straight and upright soul—
> True friend, true mate, true woman—where is She?
> True heart—as true as needle to the pole—
> True to the truth, not only true to me—
> Worth all I have to give—the best—the whole.
> When shall these eyes Her unknown beauty see? (85)

The poet in Ada Cambridge is a seeker who is on the quest—the quest for realizing the real Soul, the real Self, the real She. She is sure that she is not the body which is simply an object or form. Where is She? Where is her Soul—the true woman? She is in search of the woman who is true to truth? The outward beauty is seen but the inward beauty remains unseen. What counts for the male world is the outward beauty—an object for earning money, not the unseen inner beauty which remains of no value while it is invaluable for the woman as it is her real Self—the real Woman.

Ada Cambridge, who is straightforward in her expression, does not hesitate to call the married woman "prostitute." She believes that such married women have no right to raise their fingers against the women who are forced to sell their bodies though their hearts remain uninvolved. She feels sympathy for such women but is quite critical of the married women who blame them for immoral acts while they themselves are engaged in the immoral acts for gains. She believes that when a woman has no "bread to eat" and no "clothes to wear" because of the failure of the work, she falls low and commits sin for her life's sake. She takes this step in despair to save her life. She also takes the case of the women who, because of autumn in their lives, commit this sin for quenching the craving of the natural woman for the warmth of passion. She knows that both the cases cannot be justified on any ground. But, she raises her voices against the married women who have no right to condemn as they have opted this sin knowingly for the sake of the materialistic gains. Here are the lines which speak of Ada Cambridge's anger towards the married women who condemn the women for selling their bodies:

And who condemns? She who, for vulgar gain
And in cold blood, and not for love or need,
Has sold her body to more vile disgrace—
The prosperous matron, with her comely face—
Wife by the law, but prostitute in deed,
In whose gross wedlock womanhood is slain. (56)

The poet in Ada Cambridge believes that a married woman is a "prosperous matron" who with "her comely face" becomes "wife by the law" but in deed she becomes a "prostitute." She feels that such married woman becomes a blot as she sacrifices her 'Self' for the sake of gains for her body. The pleasure of body becomes the priority for the married woman. What she feels is that the real womanhood is locked in the wedlock. Hence, she is against the marriage which may bind the two bodies but not the two souls. Feelings are crushed under the feet of bodily pleasures.

She becomes quite critical of marriage in her poem "An Answer" which even shocked her husband. She says what she has to say. She reveals her 'Self' naturally and straightforwardly.

She feels that marriage, which should be a union of the two souls, becomes merely a means of sexual gratification. In marriage, a woman remains in chains with the feeling of bondage and slavery. It is really a poor condition that a woman has to depend on man for the nourishment of her body. The poet in Ada Cambridge is a free soul and hence does not wish to remain in fetters. What matters for her is spiritual love. Feelings matters more than the touch on the body. Man touches the body but fails to touch the soul. He does not have the hands that can touch and stir the real woman to the height. What he touches is the form in which the body of the woman resides. What is the use of the relationship which has no faith as its basis? She does not feel that marriage is essential for love. Love which arises in the heart touches the soul, even without having the physical relationship. She does not consider marriage as mandatory for love. She firmly declares that she may be his love but declines to become his wife as she does not wish to have "the yoke of servitude"—the yoke which she cannot break because of the strong fetters that play havoc on her soul. She is satisfied to have "the woman's disgrace" by remaining unmarried but she declines to commit "this old sin" of marrying, which for her is a "deep and dire mistake." What counts for her is truth and honour. For the sake of truth and honour, she will have faith—the faith that motivates her to give love to him and take love from him. She is quite aware of the love of her lover and equally she loves him with her whole heart. She will continue to give this love to him till she dies. But she reveals her apprehension that if she marries she will have to bind her 'Self' and feel as a bonded slave, the stage which she never likes to be in. It is possible that she may find a better mate or he may find a fitter mate than she is. If they are married, they cannot make a shift or cannot switch over their love to the better mate. It is not a guarantee that both of them will remain happy and blissful in their future. Some "want" or "chill" may come in between their hearts and then they cannot move to the better companion in spite of their wishes. Hence she does not wish to marry as this stage of being unmarried will make them part easily and freely from each other at the time when they wish so. Mark the lines for her frank expression and advocacy for remaining unmarried:

THY love I am. Thy wife I cannot be,
To wear the yoke of servitude....
I know thy love, and love thee all I can—
I fain would love thee only till I die;
But I may some day love a better man,
And thou may'st find a fitter mate than I;
Some want, some chill, may steal 'twixt heart and heart.
And then we must be free to kiss and part. (87)

The poet in Ada Cambridge finds the dual standard of morals for the two sexes in this male-oriented world. What she longs for is the genuine feelings of love—a kind of spiritual love that may satisfy her 'Soul', her 'Self'. She hates the idea if the lover or the husband loves only for the satisfaction of the carnal longings. She has not come in this world to satisfy the lust and bear children.

Ada Cambridge employs simple words but these words emit the fragrance of freedom—freedom from bondage and slavery whether of words, or of body, or of any. It is her language of freedom which has given a new orientation to the nineteenth century Australian poets. Her impressive phrases reveal her originality in expression—the expression which transcends the colonial world—the male monopolized world which makes the woman "twice colonized." Her frank treatment of sex, love and marriage made her the representative of the feminist movement in Australia. She proved the potential of the women authors and broke the myth of inadequacy about them.

It is the poet in Ada Cambridge who attempts to seek an answer for the honour of the fallen—the women. Her answer is that a woman is not merely a body but a soul. She has her feelings which need the companionship for sharing, not the companionship for merely bodily satisfaction—the goal which makes a man think of the body as object. What a woman needs in real sense is truth, genuine feelings and spiritual feelings of love. These are the genuine feelings towards which she makes her quest. She attempts to realize the male world that a woman is a subject with soul and not merely an object with body.

Marriage does not count as it brings the materialistic advantages in the form either of money or of respect but not of love. It is her unorthodox attitude and unconventional expressions which make her a rebel and champion for the cause of the women who long for spiritual love rather than physical one. What Saha has written about Ada Cambridge is quite true. He writes:

> By developing a discourse and style of resistance and opposition in Australian poetry towards the end of nineteenth century, Cambridge brings Australian poetry to a level of originality and maturity that transcends the narrowness of colonial pre-occupations. That Australia transforms itself from a colony to a nation by the end of the 19th century is evidenced by Cambridge's language of freedom. (60)

Works Cited

Cambridge, Ada. *Unspoken Thoughts.* http://adc.library.usyd.edu.au/data-2/v00026.pdf Web.

Encyclopaedia of Post-Colonial Literatures in English. (Eds). Eugene Benson and L.W. Conolly. New York (USA): Routledge, 2005. First published in 1994.

Saha, Subhas Chandra. "Nineteenth-Century Australian Poetry as a Mirror of Australian History: A Reappraisal." *Studies in Postcolonial Literature.* Eds. M.Q. Khan and Bijay Kumar Das. New Delhi: Atlantic, 2007. 53-61.

4

Two Nimbin (Australia) Poets: An Overview of Rob Harle and Nathalie Buckland

Jaydeep Sarangi

Rob Harle is a champion artist, poet and researcher. His writing work includes poetry, short fiction stories, academic essays and reviews of scholarly books, journals and papers. His work is published in journals, anthologies, online reviews, books and he has two volumes of his own poetry published—*Scratches & Deeper Wounds* (1996) and *Mechanisms of Desire* (2012). Recent poetry has been published in: *Rupkatha Journal* (Kolkata); *Nimbin Good Times* (Nimbin); *Beyond The Rainbow* (Nimbin); *Poetic Connections Anthology* (2013); *Indo-Australian Anthology of Contemporary Poetry* (2013); *Rhyme With Reason Anthology* (2013); *Asian Signature* (2013); *Muse India* (2014); *Voices Across The Ocean Anthology* (2014); *Episteme Journal* (2013-14); *LIRJELL Journal* (2014). His art practice involves digital-computer art both for the web and print. His giclée images have been exhibited widely. He is especially interested in promoting the inclusion of visual art in academic, scientific and literary journals. By an act of empathy, we can easily enter and exit such glorious ages that produce Bacon, Goethe, Shakespeare, Cervantes and Tolstoy, among others. His formal studies include Comparative Religion, Philosophy, Literature and Psychotherapy—his thesis concerned Freud's notion of the subconscious and its relationship with Surrealist poetry. Rob's main concern has been to explore and document the radical changes technology is bringing about. He coined the term *techno* Metamorphosis to describe this. This past concern is now moving towards helping to restore our abandoned metaphysical and spiritual modes of being through literature especially poetry.

He is currently a member of:

Leonardo Book Review Panel:

Manuscript reviewer *for Leonardo Journal;*

Manuscript reviewer for the *Journal of Virtual World Research, (USA);*

Advising Editor for the *Journal of Trans-technology Research,* (*UK*);

Advisory Editor for *Phenomenal Literature,* (*India*);

Member Editorial Board, *Episteme Journal* (*Bharat College, India*).

Member Editorial Board, *International Journal on Multicultural Literature, India*

Member Editorial Board, *LIRJELL, Lingayas University, India*

He is an important link for poetic connections between India and Australia. Rob's artwork, Publications, Reviews and selected writings are available from his website ... www.robharle.com

"He moved into the Nimbin Valley—to avoid rat-trap of metros. He converses with nature and produces an art that calms a fevered urban mind. He paints bubbles, seas, flight of sea gulls, rising suns, stars and the blue skies—infinities that can be cognized by inner eye only and not comprehended by the jet-set smart city-slickers. And since his language, idiom and syntax look foreign to them, he appears *threatening*, an outsider, a challenger, a dissident who consciously rejects the power and enticements of money, positions and awards.

He subverts the system.

He rips off the veil and shows the ugly side of the painted face! Such a guy is a *saboteur*, a dangerous figure out to challenge. Right from Plato to our tin-pot dictators, every madcap hates him as an oppositional figure out to undermine their narratives of legitimacy and authority. Rob Harle is a perpetual outsider, a wanderer, a time-traveller.

Renaissance beckons him—an age dies physically but it's fertilizing, ripe ideas continue to irrigate our souls in succeeding time sequences and timelines—as starry nights beckon artists like van Gogh or Gauguin in every age.

The age is preserved in ideas, not in its material textures." (Sharma, Boloji.com)

Tamaso Lonsdale, Nathalie Buckland, Laura Shore and Rob Harle, Rita Carter, Mark Cornell, Veronica A. Parry, Max Ryan, Mark Scrivener and Quendryth Young are important writers from Nimbin region. It's a big family and many of them publish their works in *Beyond the Rainbow*. Nimbin and surrounding areas are part of what is known as the "Rainbow Region" in Australia. Nimbin is a peaceful village that welcomes all people to enjoy. It is a vibrant place where so many talented bards live. Rob Harle and Tamaso Lonsdale have already participated in the blossoming literary ties between Australia and India. Nathalie has also contributed her poems in Indo-Australian poetic connections. Nimbin for Rob is Lake District for Wordsworth and Puri for Jayanta Mahapatra. Rob Harle is a committed artist and his commitments are in multitude."Embraced by soft music, air conditioned." For Rob Harle every word is a testimony.

Poetry is the revelation of a composite feeling that the poet believes to be social and at the same time personal which the reader recognizes as his own. Poetry for *Carl Sandburg,* is an echo, asking a shadow to dance. No matter what we touch and we wish to know about, we simply end up in the enigma that Rob Harle's words and phrases generate. Talking about the subject matter of his poetry, the Nimbin settled artist and poet Rob Harle says: "My concern is to explore the phenomenon of consciousness and our 'apparent' aloneness in this universe." Most of his poems deal with both personal and collective mosaic of experiences. As a creative artist, Harle's world revolves around art and architecture where 'Beauty is Truth and Truth Beauty'. *To Be Human* has an engaging tone and tempo in style and it deals with the modern day electronic world where humanity is getting lost into nothingness. There is a rich feast of images in Rob's poems:

"The mind deserts the body/ As electronic components flash" Rob Harle used beautiful expressions in this poem to highlight the seminal aspect of the poem:

"Our primitiveness is challenged daily/ By an insidious digital invasion." Our human universe is constantly getting challenged by the digital universe:

"This chip is God's new mask/ Enshrined in miniature." We get a glimpse of his artistic self in the poem *Nothing Ever Changes* where Rob refers to 'Van Gogh' and 'the Louvre Gallery': "...Once in a lifetime chance, to dance/ with Van Gogh and the crew from the Louvre." The modern electronic and digital universe has influenced his poetry a lot. Sometimes, he speaks in his verse of the degeneration of humanity and sometimes the superhuman power of the human being who want to cross all the limits. *The Man who would be God (A Genetic Engineer)* reverberates the theme of superhuman capacity in human beings. It resembles the Renaissance concept of 'the Vitruvian Man' who is at the centre of everything and who can conquer the whole universe from North Pole to South Pole. "He'll know from his dictionary of DNA/ His lexicon of life/the gene that makes us laugh/ The gene that makes us cry."

The use of scientific terms like 'genotype', 'DNA', 'clones', etc. proves Rob's scientific consciousness. Rob ends the poem in a fabulous way where he equals human with machine; where it is about capturing one's place by the other. *Towards A Centre* is a journey towards the centre of Creation; a journey from the state of consciousness to the state of trance: "moving forward in trance."

Deep ecology offers a philosophical basis for environmental advocacy which may, in turn, guide human activity against perceived self-destruction. Rob Harle advocates peace and order in society.

Search for Reality projects Rob's artistic consciousness where the poet's consciousness is collective. The corpus resembles the seminal theme of the poem; a journey towards 'Self'. Rob questions,

"Is life a literal or metaphoric illusion?"

Rob quotes Jonathan Livingston Seagull at the beginning of this collection: "...lost on a painted sky/ Where the clouds are hung/ For the poet's eye/ You may find me...."

The main norm for deep ecology is of self-realization and biocentric equality. The human species is a part of the Earth and not separate from it. A process of self-realisation or "re-earthing" is used for an individual to intuitively gain an ecocentric perspective. The main ethics of deep ecology are as follows—1. Richness and diversity of life forms contribute to the realization of these values and are also values in themselves. 2. Humans have no right to reduce this richness and diversity except to satisfy vital human needs. 3. The flourishing of human life and cultures is compatible with a substantial decrease of the human population. The flourishing of nonhuman life requires such a decrease. Some of Rob's poems reflect the poet's rootedness in deep ecology:

To rest in peace

The wages of a well lived life. ('Sandgate')

These lines remind me Ali Cobby Eckermann's poem, "Life is Often Silent."

When we whisk through the pages of this commendable collection we can trace out different selves of Rob—artistic, poetic, imaginative and creative.

But the gates are closed

Locked solid-topped with rusting razor wire. ('Sandgate')

Waiting makes man introspective. Writing is also inside out in words. Rob Harle is a master of doing that.

Rob Harle is a long standing friend whom I consider as a soul maker. Many of his poems reminds me Manohar Mouli Biswas. Both of them write for humanity. In the poem "Sunlight" of Manohar Mouli Biswas translated by Anandalal he expresses—

We know how to swim inside the dark room
We know how to till the field and to thresh
We know how to stay alive inside this
Ancient dark room, sniffing the smell of sweat.
Now look, the window in the east room is open
O sunlight, tell me when you'll come.

The beautiful ambiance of a poem is born out of a prophetic sensibility of the mind—a fine poem is a colourful rose that paints a feeling that it holds something more to open, even as it blooms petal by petal before the reader. A powerful poetic imagination enlivens even rusty metals and bricks; such imagination is like an intoxicating drop of wine that fuels the art of creation.

Can artwork as a therapy?

In a sense that is all it is! Given my time over again I think I would become an official art therapist, because art, more so than Freudian talking cures, psychotherapeutic sessions, etc. gets right to the heart of the matter. I was stunned by an art exhibition recently; a woman I knew 20 years ago had some mental health problems. This exhibition of abstract paintings was like looking at her naked raw psyche; with blood dripping out of the scratches after vinegar had been pored over them. It was overwhelmingly powerful, eerily beautiful and profound (Sharma, *WC*).

Are Indians better or mediocre in their Poetry? What about their hold over English? Some Western editors find it difficult to access and are known to give instant tutorials to the poets mostly professors of English only in India!

A:

I think the Indian poetry that I have been exposed to is exquisite, and as I've said before it has a more gentle 'tone' than Western poetry. There are a few 'quirky' uses of language in Indian English poetry, but that gives it its subtle nuances and charm. Any Western editor that has the audacity to 'give instant tutorials' to Indian poets, is probably both ignorant of 3 to 5,000 years of incredible history and cultural/literary/spiritual development and is perpetuating the imperialist, colonialist 'Holier than Thou' attitudes, that make them such boring ignoramuses. 'Off with their heads!' (Sharma, *WC*).

His works invite the readers with deep insights and surprise them as the foundations of the works are laid on well-researched truth and beauty.

Rob Harle contributes to human literature; literature that affirms life. He designed the cover art for the book, *The Wheel Will Turn* which has a social purpose. Manohar Mouli Biswas and many others in India are involved in literary Movement conceiving the ideology of Dr. B.R. Ambedkar: "Educate, agitate, organize". Contemporary Bangla dalit voices register a corpus of resistance to mark a journey from *nothing* to at least *something*! Rob Harle's in depth review of the dalit poet's works is exemplary. For me, Rob Harle is a harbinger of freshness in life; a friend's delight and a trusted collaborator for all seasons. Together we have produced at least five books and looking forward for more in the years to come.

Rob Harle's artistic sensibility pregnant with varied shades of feelings and emotions recollected in tranquillity. His poems capture each rainy moment of life's daily acts. He walks through long corridors of inspiring discourse through which there is often no return; but returns with the coloured wings of successive images, metaphors and poetic idioms.

If you don't already know Nathalie, you will after reading this exquisite self-expose and privileged insight into life, hers and yours.—John Bird in *Back Cover*.

Poems in Nathalie Buckland's maiden collection read naturally and consistently and are remarkably enjoyable and exciting. This enjoyment and ecstasy in the variety of subject and style is what the collection stands for. Poems appeal to our senses, we unwittingly follow a call from within. We soon become part of the poetic process and together, we move on—the poet and the reader. There is the pleasure in the recognition of a shared moment followed by a heightened awareness and anxiety. These poems can be read, studied, thought about and reveal deeper meanings of life's daily acts:

But always the sun, the sun, the sun
pulls me back
to this place of my heart, Australia,
home not of my childhood,
but of my children. ('Migrant' 3)

Nimbin and surrounding areas are part of what is known as the "Rainbow Region" in Australia. Nimbin is a peaceful village that welcomes all people to enjoy. It is a vibrant place where so many talented bards live. Rob Harle and Tamaso Lonsdale have already participated in the blossoming literary ties between Australia and India. Nathalie has also contributed her poems in Indo-Australian poetic connections. Nimbin for Nathalie is Lake District for Wordsworth and Puri for Jayanta Mahapatra. Nathalie is a committed artist and her commitments are in multitude:

Embraced by soft music, air conditioned,
paintings and subtle delicate craft
glow in poignant contrast. ("My Nimbin" 6)

Here, an indomitable gusto turns the key to a chamber of elevated thoughts. Images are woven one into another with rare brilliance and effortlessness. Nathalie, a conscious soul-maker, does not find it difficult to articulate her poetic matter into a corpus that beautifully invites her reader's interest. No matter what we touch and we wish to know about, we simply end up in the enigma that her words forge:

the log has no memory
of seed, seedling, sapling
of life as a forest giant
now felled, sliced, chopped
morphing to ash(.) ("A Fine and Private Place" 20)

One grandfather of Nathalie was a patron of famous Irish genius W.B. Yeats. Poetic inspiration for Nathalie is like 'ink in the vein'. She is an elegant poet and her language is simple and sharp:

I see her shadow
she comes

I will endure,
I am a mother. ("Daughter" 07)

The beautiful ambiance of a poem is born out of a prophetic sensibility of the mind—a fine poem is a colourful rose that paints a feeling that it holds something more to open, even as it blooms petal by petal before the reader. A powerful poetic imagination enlivens even rusty metals and bricks; such imagination is like an intoxicating drop of wine that fuels the art of creation. Nathalie's engaging lines establish her as an artist for all seasons.

Nathalie's images are both abstract and concrete. They leave things open for readers. The result is a lyrical moment of ecstasy. She shows us things from new perspectives. She reminds me of Rizio Yahanan Raj who writes about the potential, and the magic and charm of the female:

I am a woman; I posses
occult powers to breathe life
into your old coffers of whim. (*Exchanges with the Thinker,* "Wind", 24)

Like Rizio, Nathalie says, "My grail is Woman." 'Right' is a euphonious equivalent of 'might'. Nathalie follows the tradition of Gwendolyn Brooks, Sylvia Plath and Langston Hughes a 'fabric rare and strange'. Her poetic self gasps in 'chamber of maiden thoughts' to search for her emotional root proclaiming it as, sap of art is her heritage. Sap is liquid in a plant that carries food to all its parts. It is a source of vitality for the poetess to voyage within. Back cover comments are like entry keys to unfold a mysterious casket of delight. The cover design by Rob Harle adds value to the poems. As a whole, this collection is a reading wonder!

References

Biswas, Manohar Mouli. *Poetic Rendering as yet Unborn.* Kolkata: Chaturtha Dunia, 2010.

Buckland, Nathalie Shards & Figments: Poems by Nathalie Buckland, Lismore (Australia), 2013. 73.

In Conversation with Rob Harle. Sunil Sharma. *Writers in Conversation,* Vol. 1, No. 1, 2014.

The Unseen Rob Harle, Sunil Sharma Boloji.com http://www.boloji.com/index.cfm?md=Content&sd=Articles&ArticleID=15182

5

Jaydeep Sarangi in Conversation with Michelle Cahill

Jaydeep Sarangi

Michelle Cahill is an acclaimed Goan-Anglo-Indian writer who lives in Sydney, Australia. She writes poetry, fiction and essays. Her second collection *Vishvarūpa* was shortlisted in the Victorian Premier's Literary Awards. She received the Val Vallis Award and was highly commended in the Blake Poetry Prize. Her poems are anthologised in *30 Australian Poets*, Ed. Felicity Plunkett (UQP) the *Harper Collins Anthology of Modern English Poetry* Ed. Sudeep Sen, *Contemporary Australian Poets* (Turnrow) Ed. John Kinsella and *The Yellow Nib Anthology of Modern English Poetry by Indians* (QUP, Belfast) Ed. Sudeep Sen and Ciaran Carson. She was a fellow at Hawthornden Castle and Sanskriti Kendra International Retreat.

From 2013 Cahill is at the CAL/UOW International Writing Fellow at Kingston University, London. She edits *Mascara Literary Review*.

Jaydeep Sarangi: Dr. Jaydeep Sarangi has delivered lectures on diasporic literature in several continents as invited speaker/ fellow. His books on postcolonial/diasporic studies have been reviewed extensively in reputed journals in India and abroad. He edits, *New Fiction Journal* where he publishes translations of Bangala dalit literature. He is currently Associate Professor in

English, Dept. of English at Jogesh Chandra Chaudhuri College (Calcutta University), 30, Prince Anwar Shah Road, Tollygunj PO; Kolkata-700033, WB, India.

Jaydeep Sarangi can be reached at jaydeepsarangi@gmail.com

What do you consider your important works?

I don't think in terms of my work being important but I do think that establishing *Mascara* has been a significant project which has far exceeded my expectations. It has enabled me to realise my belief that language has power, influence, that language is plural and specific and that my task as a writer is to enrich and deepen the language I use for what needs to be spoken in order to disrupt the silences of various hegemonies.

When did you discover your talent for writing?

As a child I grew up in London. I would leave the smallness of our flatin Russell Square and later Chalk Farmto make my way to the bustling, grand streets of Holborn which captivated my imagination. I remember walking to and from school and just feeling inspired by a voice, a story and knowing that I would become a writer. Studying medicine was a complete digression and an escape from this, but also a confronting experience that deepened my interest in healing. Eventually, I realised that I couldn't afford to ignore my inner voice.

What are the preconditions for a good poem?

Clarity, fidelity to the experience/image that inspires it and which language embodies.

How do you structure thoughts into a poem?

Some things I have learned are to work backwards from traces of illumination to the material context, to argue against an argument, providing obstacles, to vary the tone, to distance myself from the confessional, to enable the abstract to become embedded in the language of my senses. I have also learned to be patient with ideas. To let them fertilise in my mind sometimes for months before I will allow myself to write the poem. Sometimes, poetry is best served by this postponement, at other times it demands urgency. Becoming familiar with the unpredictable and variable flows of thought and inspiration is a subtle and ongoing process.

Is there any specific significance of the title, *Vishvarūpa*?

For me the significance is that it is not an English word. That's my little triumph: as an Anglo-Indian-Goan hybrid who can barely manage a few phrases of Hindi, let alone make any kind of claim to Sanskrit. But with this book I've made *Vishvarūpa* my word.

You have written fine poems on Hindu Gods and Goddesses. Do you have a spiritual mind or does it reflect a new development within you?

Well firstly, not all the poems are spiritual. Many of them are ironic, playful, erotic or ficto-critical. The poem "Two Souls" reflects on Vedanta philosophy, embodying notions of dream, sleep, wakefulness and transcendence.

I do try to trust what I think you're describing as a 'spiritual' mind. To accept who I am and to respect those non-material needs, by which I mean a personal spiritual practice is something that I value despite neglecting it for prolonged periods. But the underlying inconsistency in Hinduism's polytheistic monotheism (non-duality) meant that I could be inventive with the Hindu pantheon as a political lens with which to interpret questions of identity, gender, power, nationality, language. This makes *Vishvarūpa* metaphorically powerful.

A large part of our identity is rooted in nationality. How has migration from one nation to another affected your identity?

I'm not sure. Maybe I have a more global, transcultural perspective than some writers. I guess I became more independent as a result of cultural transitions and travel.

How did you come to Sydney?

It was a bit like finding a publisher for the next book: a long story.

Are you a monolingual?

Pas toujours....

Do you feel to identify yourself more with any one particular nation you have stayed in so far?

I cherish the memories of my childhood and I love the landscape and other (historic-cultural) aspects of England. I feel I am Australian and yet there is disconnect which I think is about realising that Australia does not culturally embrace difference at a deep level. I am not aware of my colour in Australia but there are definitely gatekeepers. The long standing and highly entrenched White Australia Policy and various other socio-institutionalised concealed forms of racism have perpetuated homogenised white Anglo-Australian cultural facades. Australia is preoccupied with post identity but it hasn't resolved its issues of race. Writers and academics are often uncomfortable speaking about race. I might be judged for being a self-appointed activist but I'd like to ask who is judging me? When someone is threatening the status quo of course it is strategic to undermine them. That is what is happening inadvertently. I don't want to seem ungrateful since I've received a lot of support from some amazing people. There are so many gifted and forward-thinking intellectuals but unless we have these conversations in Australia, silence will prevail and change cannot take place. I know that for some people that might be happening too quickly but for many of us change is long overdue. Everything is relative. We may be born with different skin colours but speech is a shared medium, a form of equivalence so let's talk about these things. Even if nobody is talking to me but I am making them feel uncomfortable change is inevitable.

I want to mention that racism happens everywhere. In 1994 on a visit to London a woman spat in my face and told me to go 'home.' She called me a "Bengali bitch". As you can imagine that was extremely traumatic. But at the same time coming from a Christian minority, I have often felt more than a minor estrangement when I am in India or among certain Indian communities. There's nothing unusual about any of these ambivalences and provocations. Identity is complex and maybe it's impossible to define in a globalised world, and even more so for the writer, the artist who is always an exile. Besides, is it necessary for any of us to belong to one nation?

If we cherish the past I don't think too many of us can.

You also voyage into dreamscapes as a kind of Meta language of suggested meanings. Do you find this observation justified?

Dreaming suggests what lies outside and beyond it. That is what makes it as powerful as a poetic trope. In order for us to dream there must be a parallel in the real world. So dreaming is an argument if you like. It can enable political and social meanings to be suggested by the ordinary; it can persuade the reader with the intimate address of the somnambulist. It can transcend trauma, one of the pervading conditions of the colonised. And I consider the present time to be colonised in different ways to the past.

The state of dreaming is incantatory, a condition of observation more than desire, of presence as much as oblivion. It allows me to enter experience directly, knowing that the boundaries and borders are blurred, elusive and porous.

Is writing an act of resistance and emancipation for you?

Sometimes, mostly, always.... Writing is exhausting, difficult, and although it is 'the imagination pressing back against the pressure of reality' to quote Wallace Stevens, the imagination is being channelled through the writer. The writer is nothing but the vehicle so how can it be that the writer benefits? Yet, I agree with you: it is liberating to enable that process as deeply as possible. Word by word, thought by thought I try, often inadvertently, to resist the indifference of bureaucracy, the hypnosis of capitalism, the economic suppression of many kinds of colonialisms, the silencing of voiced narratives: this is the task of my writing. It might sound ambitious but why not? Why should I be co-opted into other narratives?

The most important thing for a writer to develop is a sense of their own journey. With this comes maturity. Louise Glück, a writer I deeply admire speaks of poetry being her education. We have to learn to listen to what language is teaching us: and by language I'm not talking about English or Marathi or Bengali. I'm talking about our very own words, the language we make specifically for our purpose and without which we cannot live. Only then do we begin to fulfil our potential as writers. I want to know what that feels like. I think the curse of good writing is complacency.

When creativity is unbroken a writer experiences the event happening in a very intuitive way, beyond the order of the real. This is beautiful, demanding, complex, also extremely draining and isolating. It's rare. It's like living on air. Sometimes, you know its happening because synchronicities and coincidences are happening around you. I can't always live like this but I've tasted it more than once.

Could you comment on the poetry scene in Australia?

Australian poetry is vibrant and engaged with quite a lot of emerging discussions and provocations. Of particular relevance is the eco-poetic and regional discourses, non-fiction poetry as a counter proposition to more traditional lyrical schools, the burgeoning of translations and travel poetry. The New York language schools and French symbolists have been influential in the past, as have other socio-philosophical poetic discourses. Now I think Pacific Island, South Asian and Asian Australian writing is becoming influential as we deepen our appreciation of neighbouring cultures and languages.

How vibrant is the Asian diaspora in Australia?

There has been a recent burgeoning of Asian diasporic literatures in Australia, which journals like *Peril* and *Mascara* have supported. The South Asian Diaspora in particular was celebrated in a recent symposium held in Melbourne. As well there have been many exchanges and collaborations between genres, discourses, languages within the Asian Australian diaspora. *Contemporary Asian Australian Poets*, which I co -edited with Kim Cheng Boey and Adam Aitken was published earlier this year by Puncher and Wattmann.

You edit *Mascara Literary Review* which has garnered respect by the academia and writers across the world. How is it going?

I'm proud of our achievement in human rights and cultural diversity. For these reasons *Mascara* supports a global community of writers and activists.

The problem we face is an enormous amount of administration involved, which becomes a voluntary undertaking. The future of the journal remains in crisis unless we receive core funding to pay editors and administration personnel for their time. It is a full-time job to run a literary journal and although we've received a great deal of support for which I'm immensely grateful we need to strengthen our position, be forward thinking, be strategic, be mentally composed and open to travel in new directions if the journal is going to survive.

I spent five weeks in London recently on fellowship which felt like a health retreat. I was able to renew enthusiasm because I had time for my own writing and could edit at a comfortable pace.

Do you have any special focus in the *Mascara Literary Review*?

Human rights, minority and diaspora writers, Asian Australian and Indigenous writing but overall excellent, challenged writing is a prerequisite for selection.

Publishers often consider publishing collections is a commercial suicide. How do you view this?

I have to agree.

Who are some contemporary Indian poets you have published in your magazine?

They include Keki Daruwalla, Sampurna Chattarji, Sudeep Sen, Meena Kandasamy, Dilip Chitre, Nabina Das, Anuradha Vijayakrishnan, Sukrita Paul Kumar, Rizio Rohannan Raj, Priyadarshi Patnaik, Usha Kishore, Sridala Swami, Ranu Uniyal, Srilata Krishnan as well as poets from the diaspora: the very promising Nandini Dhar, Ansley Moon, Aseem Kaul and Arjun Rajendra, Anushka Anastasia Solomon along with more established poets like Ravi Shankar, Anis Shivani, Mani Rao, Usha Akella, Lalita Noronha, Sudesh Mishra.

We have published an essay by Meena Alexander, an essay on Sujatta Bhatt by Paul Sharrad, a review by Jaydeep Sarangi of Meena Kandasamy's *Touch* at an earlier stage of her career, reviews by myself of *Language for a New Century* co-edited by Ravi Shankar and Tabish Khair's *The Gothic Post-colonialism and Otherness: Ghosts From Elsewhere*. Mridula Nath Chakraborty also reviewed *To Silence* by Tabish Khair.

We've published fiction by Ankur Agarwal, and by diasporic Indian writers: Maya Khosla, Rumjhum Biswas, A.K. Kulshreshth, and translations by the Australian poet Susan Hawthrone of Kālidāsa's *Meghadūta*.

But our interest has extended to South Asian poets more generally. For instance we published poems by the Pakistani activist, Fatima Bhutto, which are quite beautiful, deceptively simple. We also published the Pakistani-born, Californian-raised Mehnaz Turner. We've published the Sri Lankan-born Desh Balasubramaniam and from the Sri Lankan diaspora Indran Amirthanayagam has been a contributor. We have also featured an interview and poems by the Tibetan Indian writer-in-exile Tenzin Tsundue and essays and fiction by the award winning Nepalese writer Sushma Joshi.

So in answer to your question I think we have published a unique range of South Asian writers in English across a range of genres, and from several countries and cultures. What this represents I hope is an exciting hybridity. Many of these writers are multi-lingual and are connecting with more than one culture.

You are a distinguished poet and editor. Do you consider there would be any difference between a native English poet and a bilingual/trilingual poet from Asia?

Yes, of course, because they would bring to their craft different vocabularies, semantics.

You include a lot of Indian phrases and terms which are loaded with cultural nuances. Do they create thematic and linguistic distance for the native English speakers in Australia?

Without close analysis of my poems I can see why cultural nuances might be assumed. However, for several reasons I disagree with your proposition. Firstly I am using cultural terms in new contexts. The poem "Deva Loka" creates a whole new narrative embedded in myth which is being recast from my own, minority, diasporic perspective. So this be comes a contribution not an appropriation. In many poems I am speaking in the voice of a split persona, oscillating between India and Australia, between Hindu mythology and my own personal beliefs.

Also, I don't think you really need to understand every word because the process of poetry is as important as semantics and structure. I am concerned with allowing my poems to be aberrant, to take risks, to experiment with language and its possibilities. Association and implication, a resonance of multiple meanings and elusiveness are essential to my poetics so the meanings don't have to be explicit. When I read Milton I don't always understand the language and this distance is even more apparent when I read Chaucer. Moreover, many acclaimed contemporary poets write in quite a dense style, so that comprehension is clearly not the sole purpose of reading or appreciating poetry.

But also there are processes of transculturation being enacted in my poems. They are syncretic and ambulatory to a degree which is intentionally metonymic of difference and complex in its multiplicity. These are rhetorical devices; the aesthetic element is also a political manoeuvre for the kind of representation which is being staged.

And besides, I am reminded that Anglophone Australian readers are not the first Australians and that English is a lingua franca and not the native language.

Who are important reviewers/critics on you?

The best reviews, by which I mean critics who understood my craft, are by Judith Beveridge in *Westerly*, Mark Tredinnick in *Australian Book Review*, Tina Giannoukos in *TEXT*, Charles Manis in *Transnational Literature,* Tara Safranoff in *KIN and* Margaret Bradstock in *Sotto*. But I've been very fortunate with all the reviewers of my poetry. Although I respect Paul Sharrad as a critic and I published his review of *Vishvarūpa* I don't think he fully appreciated aspects of the poetics and I think there were several assumptions in his appraisal. He assumed that I work long hours as a doctor, and that therefore a lot of the poems were set at night. He also assumed that my daughter was a toddler, perhaps suggesting that I was at a different emotional stage as a mother. This had the effect of detracting from my work. It can be dangerous to bring a poet's personality or personal life into an appraisal of their craft. I think this happens more so when one is unconventional, at times provocative in one's path as a writer, as I have been.

Is there an anxiety to portray Indianness in your writings?

I don't think so. My poem "Mumbai By Night" breaks many non-secular taboos (drugs, sexuality), that would otherwise be considered to characterise a traditional kind of identity. But it goes further. The poem anarchically revels in the wreckage and clefts of a postcolonial identity. I don't think that could be a striving to portray Indianess and I am aware that many Indian readers would disapprove. Rather, I want to assert my identity, inscribe it unashamedly as something unique in this poem.

So it's a poem that speaks of *un-heimlich*, of not belonging to a city, even a family yet somehow being familiar, in-between. I have tried to be as ruthless as I can about the truth if you like of my story. But sometimes I cannot. I think "Shaping the Linga' is the most elusive poem in that collection but I think this is signalled to the reader as an intentional strategy that the speaker employs. That is a sensible thing to do, sometimes.

What do you suggest for budding young poets from Australia and India?

Write. Keep writing and don't stop. Language, I would say, is quite possibly the answer to its own problems.

What's your immediate wish?

To accept the utterly uncompromising truth of being a writer.

Thank you, Michelle! Wishes for your future projects!

6

Kevin Gilbert's Aboriginal Verse: An Epitome of Uniform Justice

Darkhasha Azhar

Kevin Gilbert, globally famous for his aboriginal verse, was committed to a life sentence over the killing of his wife during an argument. The episode sounds strange but speaks volumes about his personal life and its obvious effect on his literary skill. While in prison Gilbert took up writing. In 1968, he started to pen the play '*The Cherry Pickers*' which was smuggled out of jail on toilet paper. The play was readily accepted and admired. The similarity between his crime and his parents' death are remarkable and they do not go unnoticed by him. In his poem entitled '*Think*' Gilbert wrote about the parental link:

> My father was a white, He killed his wife
> She was a half-caste, She was my mother.
> I am a half-caste, I killed a white
> She was my wife. (*New lit...Gupta,* 82)

Gilbert was the product of an English father and an aboriginal mother. The mixture of white and black parentage and investigation of relationships between them were the themes in his writings. The poem '*Inhabitant of the Third World*' deals with the treatment of a half caste Aboriginal. He wrote simple poems in his collection of children's poetry to communicate his feeling of family to all children. Throughout his writings Aboriginal mythology is continually used affirming his ties to his people. He is often found making reference to '*Ba' aime*—the Aboriginal god or supreme spirit. Other generalized concepts include '*gubbah, baccadul, gin, goom* and *boori*. These general words or mythological references are used to identify these poems as uniquely aboriginal, adding authenticity. He does not edit or correct the language demonstrating the true characteristics of Aborigines as if speaking with them face to face. His poetry contains misspoken words that emphasise the speech pattern. The best example of this style is his collection *People Are Legends* published in 1978.

Gilbert is often billed as the first Aboriginal playwright to have his work performed. Gilbert's play is based on the stories and experiences of itinerant workers and it deals with spiritual searching and loss faced by his people pushed into refugee situations and desocialisation. The play's narrative mixes traditional creation—myths, rituals, political diatribes, clever dialogue and humour to bring forth the genuine effect. It is through this humour that Gilbert explores alcoholism, violence and spiritual and cultural issues. From 1972 onwards Gilbert was active in numerous Aboriginal human rights causes. He also authored *Because a White Man'll Never Do It* in 1973. In 1972, another play by Gilbert, *The Gods Look Down*, is poetic and semi-abstract and moves from dialogue accompanied by movement to movement-based on explorations of love and sexuality.

In his early verse, Gilbert uses the poetry as an apologia in respect to his own life whilst challenging the morality of the wider society. The author considers the political involvement and stance as well as the particular social conditions in which they live—which is often addressed in their work. The initial critical reception of his work was hostile partly because it was something new and different on the Australian literary scene, something which did not conform to canons of poetic acceptability as they had been devised by the White Australian intelligentsia. Despite technical flaws, it is a verse which is intended to be read out loud and always gains added power when it is delivered in this way. The most important aspect of Gilbert's writing is that he introduced an Aboriginal perspective into contemporary Australian literature for the first time. He celebrated Aboriginal survival in the face of adversity, lamented prejudice and oppression, and offered an optimistic view of the potential for interracial harmony in the country. Gilbert was a pioneer in a new form of Australian poetry, embracing directness, environmental values and an overriding Aboriginal world view.

Gilbert writes about Aboriginals who had their own societies, cultures and religions. The land which belonged to them was managed, nurtured, protected and respected by Aboriginal people in a cyclic process of renewal and reformation. For them the land was the core of all individuality, spirituality, identity and purpose. When the British first Colonized Australia they claimed that the land was owned by no one. It was on this basis that they snatched the country from the original owners and formed their own government. It was within six months that they destroyed a way of life. In every way, the Aboriginals were humiliated, exploited and neglected. They were deliberately pushed into the quagmire of poverty and subjected to an unnatural death. Consequently, the Aboriginal's right to land and the struggle to obtain recognition and compensation for land are Gilbert's most prominent themes. The Aboriginal culture and identity are expressed in his poem "The Blackside". He highlights the influence of white society on the realm of Aborigines in the poem "The Spirit of Progress" and describes as well as criticises the emerging commercialism:

> Abos! Photos!
> Buy a spear, Buy a boomerang!
> Bark art here! How much?
> Pay him! A dollar do?
> Twenty cents! He don't eat like you
> he's an Abo; don't need much
> wastes it all on wine and such!
> Don't need tucker; It's all in bush goanna,
> Grubs and nardoo mush! Dirty Abo! (Gupta, *New Lit...*, 83)

Gilbert criticised white Australia in his writing by attacking the white men in his poem *Aboriginal Query* which brings together all his thoughts about white society and their exploitation of Aborigines:

> What is it you want Whiteman?
>
> What do you need from me?
>
> You have taken my life, My culture, My dreams
>
> You have leached the substance of love from my being.... (Gupta, *New Lit...,* 83)

Kevin Gilbert's poetry is remarkable for its directness. It shows much concern for Aboriginal social issues and he also brings a greater daring, a greater appreciation of Black Australian. His poems "The Gurindji", "Look", "Koori", and "Roll of Drums" stress the need for Aborigines to continue to fight for justice otherwise they will always remain unrecognized. In *The Roll of Drums*, Gilbert is adamant about all Aborigines standing up and fighting injustice and discrimination. This poem raises one of the most important aspects of Gilbert's literary work—his blunt description of truth. The truth may have offended some but it was the best means of making whites aware of the position of Aborigines in Australian society.

Gilbert's poetry has been enthusiastically received in some quarters and viewed with disfavour in others. For example, one critic enthused that *People Are Legends* '*consists of metrical poems that flash and sparkle like polished gemstones*' (Gil Perrin, Songs...Journal, 6) while another complained that *'often the language is stiff and mannered, and nowhere more so than in the title poem, whose good deal of truth does not cover up its verbal shallowness, facile twists of bitter wit, self-defeating bluntness, and carelessness of prosody'* (Peter Monaghan, *Fruits...,* 15). In a sense, such a wide range of opinion is to be expected concerning poetry which is so accusatory and disconcertingly direct. Gilbert certainly does not mince his words, as some of his more striking openings attest:

> I've had a cunt of a life
>
> I suppose
>
> As a woman. (Gilbert, Riches, *People Are...,* 17)

And:

I'll sell me moot for half a note
And a bottle of wine if you need. (Gilbert, "The Other Side", 11)

And finally: he just as forthrightly takes the reader to task:

But I reckon the worstest shame is yours
You deny us human rights. (Gilbert, "Shame", 13)

While Gilbert can stir feelings of culpability in sensitive White Australian readers, many would dismiss his stance as anti-white racism. But a careful reading of Gilbert's verse makes it impossible to maintain this view. For he is just as critical of Black Australians who allegedly sell out their people by accepting European accolades or well-paid government employment, or by passive complacency. Some of the author's most trenchant verse is aimed at these supposed betrayers of the Aboriginal movement. For example, the clipped line length and powerful rhyme scheme in "The Better Blacks" is most effective:

Watch for the traitors
Dressed in black
Watch for those jackies
Up you Jack!
Watch for the puppet
Watch for the brute
Living like a whiteman
Grey serge suit. (Gilbert, "The Better Blacks", 26-27)

There is no clearer example of Gilbert's ability to rankle others than the aftermath of his caustic poem, "To My Cousin, Evonne Cawley", given pride of place in "The Bulletin Literary Supplement" of September 1980:

I wonder, Evonne, when you're playing straight sets
And you 'haste' your opponent so well,
Do you ever look back at your grandmother, black
And catch glimpses of her in her hell? (Gilbert, 2)

The publishers of *The Bulletin*, Consolidated Press, were put in an awkward position when the poem they had highlighted in their advertising for this issue prompted Cawley to undertake ultimately successful legal action against them. Not only did this demonstrate Gilbert's ability to raise indignation through his verse; it was also an excellent example of the potential social impact of Aboriginal literature, of the convergence of poetry and political considerations. Gilbert says that he has adopted writing as a means of voicing the Aboriginal situation and tried to present as truly as possible the Aboriginal situation and the Aboriginal response. He strongly felt the need to educate White Australians to the present situation of Aboriginal people presenting it as honestly as possible because the picture that surfaced was not ugly.

Though there is a strong, militant side to Gilbert's often sarcastic poetry, there is another side of it which most Australians are not aware of. Even in *People Are Legends*, a sense of sardonic humour emerges in such poems as "Granny Koori", in which Gilbert portrays the symbolic emasculation of Aboriginal men:

> Dear Director of Aboriginal Grants
> My association needs $55,000 bucks
> To purchase silky black ladies pants
> A quota to cover each area, the Territories—
> State by state
> To conceal from the prying eyes of the world
> The Aborigines poor buggered fate. (42)

Gilbert's vibrant humour is often disguised in his poetry, but is particularly evident in his drama. There is a further facet to Gilbert's talent which encompasses most of his unpublished material. He has written a number of very different poems, still only in manuscript form, which celebrate such themes as love and devotion. If one examines an unpublished poem such as "Extract from a Letter to a Woman Friend", one might not believe it was written by the same man who produced *People Are Legends*:

> And I would part the weeping willows
> Hold the birch firm in my hand

Gently stroke the living waters
Whispering to the fertile land
Beams of sunshine shot with silver
Thriving brown and vital hue
Resting land aglow with nature
Dreaming of the ever you. (*MSS*, 2429)

Gilbert has also written a substantial series of whimsical and light poems in the form of nursery rhymes entitled "Kids Poems" directed at children, but again, these exist only in unpublished form:

Once I met a mad Rosella
He was quite a crazy fella
Who got drunk on nectar-ferment
From a rich old bottle-brush
His wings he flapped and fluttered
While foolishly he muttered
I wish I was an eagle
Or a fine plumed English thrush. (*MSS*, 2584)

Many of these poems deserve publication; however, the variety of Gilbert's accomplishments has been downplayed both by the media and by publishers, thereby perpetuating his image as solely a 'protest' poet. This is primarily because, in Gilbert's words, "publishers didn't want my love poetry" (*Personal interview*). It seems to be commercially more profitable to publish a militant Aboriginal writer than to print less controversial material. Therefore, Australian publishers have dictated the public image with which well-known Aboriginal authors have been cloaked.

One wonders whether Les Murray's rather unjust review of *People Are Legends* might have been different if all the dimensions of Gilbert's poetic achievement had been represented in the book. Murray commented, "Worst of all, he confuses vehemence with poetic intensity. Unlike many radical versifiers, he has things to be vehement about, but poetry will not be forced" ("In Search...", 16). Some of Gilbert's work is awkward in terms of meter and scansion. But some of his most fluid verse is that which relies upon an ear for Aboriginal colloquial speech and intonations, as in *The Gurindji:*

> Poor fellow
> Simple fellow
> Sweet fellow
> Strong
> Sittin' in the desert
> Singin' desert song
> Cryin' countin' chickens
> Chickens made of lan'
> Poor fellow
> Silly fellow
> Sad fellow
> Cry
> White fellow gibbit lan'
> To hide you when you die. (44-46)

Above all else, Aboriginal poetry is remarkable for its striking immediacy, which is often augmented by the personal or political stance of the author. It is this factor which conveys it's political, literary and its colloquial, oral and phonetic strength. While Aboriginal poetry underscores the Fourth World dimension of the Black Australian situation, it highlights at the same time the distinctive Aboriginal world view in Australia. In the introduction to his landmark anthology of Aboriginal poetry, *Inside Black Australia*, Kevin Gilbert highlights most eloquently the independent paradigm of black verse:

> Black poets sing, not in odes to Euripides or Dionysus, not Keats, nor Browning, nor Shakespeare; neither do they sing a pastoral lay to a 'sunburnt country' for they know that the russet stain that Dorothea Mackellar spoke of is actually the stain of blood, our blood, covering the surface of our land so the white man could steal our land. (156)

Works Cited

Gilbert, Kevin. "People Are Legends". Mitchell Library, 1970.

——. *People Are Legends*. St. Lucia, 1978.

——. "People Are Legends" in *End of Dreamtime*. Sydney, 1971.

——. "Riches", "The Other Side of the Story", "The Flowering", "Shame", "The Better Blacks", "Granny Koori" in *People Are Legends*.

——. "To My Cousin Evonne Cawley". *The Bulletin Literary Supplement*. September, 1980.

——. "Extract from a Letter to a Woman Friend", *Poems 1970*. Mitchell Library, 1970.

——. Untitled Verse, 'Kids' Poems'. National Library of Australia, 1979.

——. 'Introduction', *Inside Black Australia: An Anthology of Aboriginal Poetry*. Ringwood, 1988.

——. *The Cherry Pickers*. Canberra: Burrambinga Books, 1988.

——. *The Gods Look Down and Other Sketches*. Self-published. Sydney, 1990.

Monagham, Peter. "Fruits of Oppression." *The Canberra Times*. 27 May, 1979.

Murray, Les A. "In Search of a Poet". *The Sydney Morning Herald*. 7 October 1978.

Personal interview with Kevin Gilbert. Canberra. May, 1981.

Perrin, Gil. "Songs of Protest and Rural Poems". *Village News and NALA Journal*. 6 September, 1978.

7

Reflections on Eco-criticism in Judith Wright's Poetry

Neeta

Eco-criticism is relatively a new branch of literary criticism and the term was for the first time used by William Rueckert in his essay "Literature and Ecology: An Experiment in Eco-criticism", Published in 1978. Later, with the publication of two famous books *The Eco-criticism Reader* edited by Cheryll Glotfelty and Harold Fromm and *The Environmental Imagination* by Lawrence Buell, in 1996, the term started to be much discussed and debated. The theory of Eco-criticism evolved as a result of development of new consciousness that very soon "There will be nothing beautiful (or safe) in nature to discourse about, unless we are very careful" (P.K. Nayar, *Literary Theory Today*, 291). Motivated by the idea of saving the environment from total chaos, a number of creative writers started to express their concerns about the world which is much burdened by the wide spread ecological crisis and used Eco-criticism to bridge the gap between literature and environment. They started to use literature as a medium to articulate their views and to sensitize the reader towards the ecological crisis. Judith Wright, the celebrated Australian poet is one of them.

Besides being a poet, Judith Wright is also famous as a short story writer, critic, environmentalist and social activist. She composed poetry with a motive as she believed that the poet should be concerned with his social and natural surroundings.

She was well aware about the rift that had developed between man and nature owing to the changed attitude of man. Pointing out the theme of Judith Wright's, *The Two Fires* (1995), M.C. Kinney writes that the recent change in the attitude of man is the outcome of "the conception, on one hand, of Nature as a self-sufficient physical system which is essentially the counterpart of a sensory experience, and on the other of man, the triumphant investigator of the ultimate secrets of this external physical system, as the master of his own intellectual and material destiny. It is this dual idea that has constituted the inspiration of our whole modern way of life, and the significant fact is that, at the point where the latter conception that of man as the master of his own destiny has come to dominate our minds" (Mckinney, 105).

Though her life was disrupted by a society in conflict, she always wished to harmonize life at personal, social and ecological nature on an internal level. She has herself asserted:

> The landscape I knew was full of a deep and urgent meaning...these hills and plains...these rivers and plants and animals were what I had to work with as a writer, and they themselves contained the hidden depths of a past beyond anything that cities and the British invasion had to offer. (Judith Wright, 51)

Her collections are replete with poems which expose and examine the contemporary social and national scenario. Her poetry reflects her commitment mainly to environment and the right of indigenous people of Australia. Environmental degradation owing to millennium's pressure of rapid growth of industry, science and technology and population pained her like an eco-critic and through her creativity she laid bare the realistic picture before her readers in such a way that they might be compelled to think about forces, gradually devastating nature. She never liked anthropocentric views of man's separation from his environment and she expressed her reactions to it in a number of poems and critical articles. When she was once asked if she considered herself to be a nature poet, she replied:

> No, I don't. My real interest, I think, is the question of man in nature, man as a part of nature. The theory of correspondence

> that Baudelaire brought forward, the question of nature as a symbol of one's experience has always seemed to me to have a great deal in it. (Thompson, 73)

Obviously Judith Wright thinks that balance on this planet can be maintained only by proper co-existence of man and nature. In a way, she believes in unity of all things existing on the planet. In her opinion, earlier pagan nature religion may offer a good model for our nature protection.

She has a passion for protection of environment and in her work; she expresses her concern about deforestation, sand mining, soil erosion, etc. Trees are the major part of the scheme of nature and these are not only very essential to the fulfilment of human needs but also contribute in the plan of nature by interacting with earth, birds, animals, air and life as a whole in this world. Thus, these maintain a connectedness with earth. Man in his futile attempts to make progress is devastating forests by uprooting a number of trees.

In her poem "Rain Forest" she describes insensibility of human beings in appreciating beauty of nature in the "Rain Forest". Though in the poem beauty of nature has been described from the point o view of tree—frog yet it is full of greater meanings:

> We with our quick dividing eyes
> Measure, distinguish and are gone
> The forest burns, the tree frog dies,
> Yet one is all and all are one. ("Rain Forest")

In one stanza the poet has described the perception of nature in Frogs mind as "all is one and one is all." It means all are equal no matter, whether one belongs to a particular species or the other. Though in the end of the poem everything is destroyed but it has been destroyed together as an entity. In that respect both frog and python are the same. In the next stanza, she describes the attitude of men who has "quick dividing eyes", towards nature and observes his existence more important than others. His decisions are rash and logical but these are not always true and prove to be the best. He is in capable of understanding the consequences of the outlook that segregates him from nature.

In a way Judith Wright like a true eco-critic emphasizes oneness of nature's plan in which man is merely an entity. Judith Wright maintains that behind the environmental degradation, man's inattentive and heedless attitude is responsible. Human cynicism which is there simply to analyze and criticize is useless; rather measures should be taken to seek connection with all that is good and reasonable. The line "yet one is all and all are one" no doubt, hints at the unifying approach which Judith Wright wants man to have but it also implies if one thing is destroyed everything would automatically be destroyed.

Scribbles on Smooth white trunks of Australian gum trees are a common sight. Though scientifically it is a proven work of an insect, Judith Wright is capable of reading the meaning of life in it. She finds human beings, missing in their approach to learn the deep meanings of life in these scribbles and other objects of nature.

> The gum tree stands by the spring
> I peeled its splitting bark
> And found the written track
> Of a life I could not read. ("Scribbly Gum")

Human approach to consider nature senseless and merely an entity to be subservient to human needs has made life misbalanced on this planet.

Destruction and devastation of land in the wave of progress has been criticized by her in the poem "Jet Flight over Derby".

> And therefore, when land dies
> Opened by whips of greed
> These plains lie torn and scarred
> Then I erode; my blood
> Reddens the stream in flood. ("Jet Flight over Derby")

Greed of man to put himself in the realm of progress is responsible for the degradation of environmental conditions. Man has been presented as an oppressor and nature sighs like a sufferer under the severe punishment given to her. The poet, like an eco-critic condemns this behaviour of human beings. The words of Moore in relation to Judith Wright's views about the treatment of nature are quite apt:

> Nature can no longer be viewed as a machine. It has a living aspect, with which we find ourselves identifying. We can perceive, in the change from day to night, from winter to spring, an inescapable correspondence with the process of our own bodies, and we can see those same changes going on in creatures other than ourselves...so it was this revived sense of correspondence between man and his world that revitalized poetry in early nineteenth century. (Moore, 67)

The major issue to be discussed today is the protection of environment which largely depends on the attitude of man towards nature. Man's arrogance to consider him to be powerful enough to break all laws of nature is merely his ignorance. Judith Wright criticizes such an attitude and appeals for a change in it. Nature should be considered a living entity equally important and powerful in total scheme of life.

The poem "Eroded Hills" from the collection *The Gateway* describes the drastic changes that have taken place in the landscape of the New England table land in the name of progress.

> These hills my father's father stripped
> And beggars to the winter wind
> They crouch like shoulder naked and whipped
> Humble, abandoned, out of mind. ("Eroded Hills")

For the purpose of disused mine shaft, nature is being disrobed. Generations after generations are engaged in causing devastation but as a sensible human being, she suffers from a sense of guilt as it has been done by "my father's father". For such an attitude of man, "she often uses images of man 'taming' and 'exploiting' the landscape highlighting its vulnerability, its 'femininity'" (*The Age*, 19). The attitude of Australians is that the land is there to be raped. Disrobing of nature has been condemned by the poet. In the poem, she also pleads for replanting trees to overcome the harm done to the hills. The mistake which has been committed by my father's father i.e. our ancestors should definitely be amended by us. For her trees are the major component of the ecosystem on which the existence of whole of the diversity of species depends.

> I rather think that she saw the trees as natural corollaries to the any kinds of birds she wrote about in their diversity, their resilient struggle for life in difficult circumstances and in their silent contribution to the ecosystem we all breathe. (Smith, 1)

Judith Wright though thinks like an eco-critic of modern age, her thinking leads her to be considered as a mystic. She has herself asserted that anyone who does the deep thinking about a place of man in nature would lead on the same path as the mystic have. Her poem "Cycads" stands in true testimony of it. Here she attempts to make man understand that he has to learn from the trees.

> Take their cold seed and set it in the mind,
> And its slow root will lengthen deep and deep
> Till, following, you cling on the last ledge
> Over the unthinkable, unfathomed edge
> Beyond which man remembers only sleep. ("Cycads")

Seed of virtue should be sown in the mind of men where it would lie dormant for sometimes and grow silently till its own age so that he may learn the secret of cycad tree to be happy and full of warmth even in the old age. In her yet another poem "Woman to Child", she describes the scheme of nature in the following words.

> I am the earth, I am the root.
> I am the stem, that fed the fruit,
> The link that joins you to the night. ("Woman to Child")

She stresses the point that man should try to understand the plan of nature as a whole, not in bits because the practical knowledge of it may prove dangerous not only to him but also to other creatures, living on the earth.

In her poem "The Hunting Snake", she clearly differentiates snake's purpose of hunting and man's purpose of killing varied animals of nature. When the snake is aiming at his prey, he focuses on the prey—"Head down", tongue flickering on the trail, then the poet describes the movement. "He quested through the parting grass" the use of the word "quested" is quite significant and through it, she wants to convey the idea that snake is having a quest like a true worshipper (seeker) of truth. It means it is his mission at the moment, especially to sustain its life but man's efforts to kill nature can never be justified as these are mission less and motivated by his sense of possession and superiority. The poet at the level of eco-criticism compels the readers to think about the position of snake and man in the food chain of the ecosystem. Both of them are integrated part of it but their behaviours are quite different. The scene of departing snake has been portrayed by the poet as "cold, dark and splendid he was gone", indicating that after competition of his mission, he feels satisfied and departs calmly from the place but human behaviour, just as an observer reveal that they are not much satisfied with such a behaviour so they "looked at each other." Use of the phrase "went on" at the end of the poem signifies man's sense of continued passion for possession.

Her "Sanctuary" is a poem which depicts a rift between citizen from urban area and peace of forest symbolizing nature. The very title of the poem has an ironic implication and hints at the thoughtlessness of human efforts. Development done in the name of progress by clearing away lands indicates the bleak future of Australia. The poem depicts the scene of a night in which the driver of a car speedily moving on the wet—road which stands symbolically for human progress. In a usual manner he easily passes the sign where the word "Sanctuary" has been written—

> Off the side of the road there is:
> The immense/tower of antique forest and life, the rock
> Where years accumulate like leaves, the tree
> Where transient birds and mindless insects sing.
> ("Sanctuary")

The poetess has clearly shown the undisturbed atmosphere of the "Sanctuary" in the poem by using the insects, antique forests, transient birds, etc. The driver of the car does not pay even the least attention towards that board because he believes

"Only the road ahead is true/ it knows where it is going, we go too". Such a disconcerted behaviour of the driver symbolizes the unconcerned attitude of modern man towards nature. The driver only observes the road ahead and drives car on it to wherever it is going. It is quiet ironical that the road does not known where it is going but he solely depends on it. Ultimately at the end of the poem Judith Wright writes that the road "Lands into the world cities like a long fuse laid." Through this line she suggests that such a mentality as this driver has would lead to a complete destruction of human race, if men are unobservant about nature and its surroundings. In a way, it can be said that Judith Wright like an analytical observer of nature predicts the future of humanity in this post-modern world depending more on science and technology, forgetting the cardinal relationship of man and nature. Whenever Judith Wright observes the collapsed systems and environmental degradation, she used to brood over possible reasons and at a number of times points out that there is an urgent need of developing a new way of understanding the relationship between man and nature. She always puts a question mark on the attitude of man towards nature. Man's wish to have dominion over the land and to utilize its resources to the utmost of its capacity, his presumption to have a command over nature compelled the poet to comment on the evil consequences of such behaviour. Through her poems she always tries to show the path of awareness to the human beings.

In the poem "Australia 1970", she expresses her anger on the insensible use of land and nature by human beings. She criticizes the belief that through technology and science, man can solve all his problems. She expresses the need of an urgent and committed action so that environmental protection may be assured:

> For we are conquerors and self-prisoners
> More than scorpion or snake
> And dying of the venoms that we make
> Even while you die of us. ("Australia 1970")

Man has considered himself to be the conqueror and under the intoxication of his power and position he has forgotten the pious terms and conditions of living together with nature. In spite of being well known about the fact that his existence solely depends on the safe existence of nature, he is ready to harm it. Judith Wright purposefully makes attempts to compel people to think about nature in better and different terms. Her artistic instinct makes her capable of understanding the things surrounding her in a better way and she could also express those ways to her readers in an emphatic manner. Her queer combination of the poet and an activist provide her with an opportunity to express her views on current environmental crisis in Australia in particular and the world in general. As an artist, she has a deeper and broader view to look at the problem and as an activist, she could boldly convey these ideas to the general public that the means adopted by modern man are self-destructive.

Her poem "Unknown Water" has been composed with a view to express water crisis in Australia. In the poem, she imagines the absence of water on land and a sense of fear owing to this absence. Drying rivers, lakes and other fresh water sources of Australia are the focus of her attention. The poem has been written in the narrative style. The poem narrates the story of an old man who lost one of his foals because of draught, in spite of the fact that he is well versed about cattle and all livestock. In the second stanza, the narrator reveals the fact that she knows the water hole that never drives "Even the sons and daughters have forgotten".

> ....you can understand that;
> You lived by water not like the cattle drank,
> But the water you known of is dried up now. All dried,
> And the drought goes raging on. Your own sons and daughters
> Have forgotten what it is to live by a water
> That never dries up. But I know of another creek.
> You will not understand my words when I tell of it.
> ("Unknown Water")

These lines depict drought blighted earth and the sufferings of human beings in absence of water. The "old man" in the poem represents traditional thinking and accustomed tradition. At the end of the poem she optimistically tells to go easy with me, old man, "I am helping to clear a track to unknown water." This insistence on hearing a track of unknown water suggests a new consciousness she wants to inculcate in the modern man so that they start to think nature, not as subservient to human needs but having an integrated entity with human life. Judith Wright emphasizes that at the time of environmental crisis, there is an acute need to research the lost roots of human relationship with nature. Forgetfulness of the daughters and sons is suggestive of negligent and unmindful attitude of modern man towards the traditional approach of nature.

Obviously, the poems of Judith Wright are expressive of her concern for the current environmental crisis, faced by the planet. She considers the changed attitude of man towards nature, the main cause for it. Man passion for progress, pride to consider his existence superior to the existence of nature and his cynicism simply to analyze and criticize whole phenomenon of nature have challenged the concept of unity of all things existing on this planet. In the words of Stephen Harris: "For Judith Wright, the degradation of the environment by human beings is a distressing symptom of the human disconnection and separation from the natural world. Through her poetry and political activism, she envisioned a healing of this disjunction, a return to the unity of human and world to be achieved through the fostering of a transformative new knowledge—a new way of being gained through the transformation of the separate individual self so integral to our western notion of being" (Stephen, 11, 20). She is of the opinion that the future of the planet largely depends on man's attitude towards it. Therefore he has to develop a kind of relationship with nature in which oneness of all things, present on the planet may be assured.

Works Cited

Harris, Stephen. "Narratives from Another Creek: Judith Wright and the Poetics of Water in Australia", *Journal of Eco-criticism* 1 (2), July 2009.

Mckinney, *The Challenge of Reason*. Brisbane: The Mountain Press, 1950.

Moore, "The Quest of Judith Wright" reprinted in A.K. Thomson, *Critical Essays on Judith Wright*. Jacarnda, 1968.

Nayar, Pramod K., *Literary Theory Today*. New Delhi: Asia Book Club, 2006.

Smith, Greg, "We are Turned into a Great Tree: Judith Wright's Strange Word about Trees" in *Australian e-journal of Theology*. June 2006.

Thompson, "Poetry in Australia: Judith Wright", reprinted in Brian Kiernan (eds.) *Considerations*. Sydney: Angus and Robertson, 1977.

West, Rosemary (ed.), "Eve Alone in her Garden" in *The Age*, 27 June 1986.

Wright, Judith and Patrick White, "The Story of Australia, *Going on Talking*" in *Butterfly Books*, Springwood, NSW, 1992.

The poems have been quoted from *Wright J: Collected Poems 1942-1985*. Sydney: Angus and Robertson, 1998 and have been incorporated in the body of text with the name of poems.

8

The Waste Land and *The Living and the Dead*: A Utopian Perspective

Meenu Dubey

He was a serious, not necessarily a solemn man, a severe man, never lacking in kindness and sympathy, a profound man. And yet outward appearance a correct man, a conventional man, an infinitely polite man—in brief a gentle man. He was not only incapable of a mean deed; I would also say that he never had a mean thought. He could mock folly and he was server with sin, and there were people he simply did not wish to know. But his circle of friends, though never very large, was very diverse, and he could relax with great charm in the presence of women. He had moods of gaiety and moods of great depression—I have known occasions when I left him feeling that my spirit had been utterly depleted. Often he was witty (in a somewhat solemn voice): his anecdotes were related with great deliberation.... In personal habits he was scrupulously correct and clean, never a Bohemian in thought or appearance; but he had a streak of hypochondria, and was addicted to pills and points. I never saw him indulge in any sport.... He made a fetish of umbrellas...had them especially made with enormous handles, with excuse that no one would take such an umbrella from a cloakroom by mistake. He relished good food and beer and wine, but his specialty was cheese of which he had tasted a great many varieties. (Herbert, Read, 36-37)

Above quoted remark describes T.S. Eliot as an 'invisible poet' who was one of the great worthies consorting with his peers in the realm of Letters.

> *Times Literary Supplement* mentioned for *The Living and the Dead*
>
> It is a second novel, rarefied in temper, fastidious in sensibility, often Subtle in intellectual perception, the work of an anxious and acutely word conscious mind. Mr. White's style is tricky and individual, though also curiously misty and bloodless.

Talking of the influence of T.S. Eliot on his early works especially Patrick White himself wrote:

> Joyce and Lawrence, yes at the time when I began to write. I certainly began to read Dostoevsky about the same time, and have read all his important novels, but it would not have occurred to me that I had been influenced by anybody so remote from myself, geographically understand his temperament fairly well. Most certainly I shouldn't have made use of the stream of consciousness if it hadn't for Joyce. (Bjorksten 3)

Above quote justifies that Patrick White share the fear of Eliot's belief that a modern man's life is out of joints for the springs of spiritual nourishment as he is assured that they are lost and over, even while they survived Australian Noble Prize laureate Patrick White belong to the tradition of novelist like Dostoevsky, Tolstoy, Lawrence and Joyce. Like them he also tried to probe into the "epic vision of life", 'man's place in the Universe', 'mankind's eternal quest' for and a 'value in existence'. Patrick White is the best known Australian novelist. He is ranked among the best in the world literature he won recognition as a playwright. Short story writer also in fact he is the first significant writer who identified himself with Australian Social and intellectual outlook. His regulation dated from the appearance of *The Tree of Man* (1955). His *Voss*, *Riders in the Chariot*, *The Solid Mandala* and *A Fringe of Leaves* are the works of repute.

He is one of the most popular writers among Indian studies and tastes for literatures of the world. His second novel *The Living and the Dead* influenced by T.S. Eliot's *The Waste Land* to a large extent.

It is a serious family novel. The action of the novel is coloured by the central political conflict of the Spanish Civil war but the novel covers the entire history of war and its misery. Patrick White well enough to enthrall with his language alone.

It is a novel of Paralysis and Senseless sacrifice, love, death and politics of the thirties; it is a curious document of a certain milieu and times.

His fiction campaigns against false hopes of happiness and the perils of seeking it in sex, power and possessions for him, intense happiness is to be found in marriage, work integrity even purity (Marr Monthly, 32).

The Novel *The Living and the Dead* set in London, revolves around the brother and Sister Elyot and Eden Standish and their mother, Catherine. The three Standish are complicated figures, not necessarily naturally aloof but ultimately driven to stand apart. The mother was born Kitty Goose, transformed by marriage into Catherine Standish. Her husband is no saviour, however. Her situation is improved, but not convincingly, and her spirit is quickly and decisively broken. The husband is a failure, and he fails at the marriage as well, leaving Catherine to raise the two children.

Elyot is a writer and critic, provided for by a small trust. He is devoted to his books, "a devotion to the dust," as White describes it. Elyot studies in Germany and at Cambridge, gaining experience and yet finding himself apart. "It began to occupy him more and more, his not being part of anything," but he is unable to change his conditions.

His sister, Eden, is more of a free spirit, though that is only a manifestation of her own search for meaning. She turns to polities, and to men, suffering also for her choices.

Other figures include Connie Tiarks, a childhood acquaintance of the Standish' who later becomes a friend and remains close to the family over the years. She loves Elyot, but it is a love that is not meant to be.

The strongest character is Joe Barnett, a working class man involved with Eden (and admired by Elyot). He decides that he must fight in the Spanish Civil War; there fate has its way with him.

Elyot, in contrast, is almost completely unable to act, stumbling even into his career.

What this paper seeks to find out is how a strong parallel co-relation runs between *The Waste Land* and *The Living and the Dead*. Both works saturate the theme of sterility and spiritual starvation in the life of modern man. Patrick White follows the structural pattern adopted by Eliot to explore his vision.

Just as Tiresias speculates on life gliding off into memory, Elyot ruminates on the past. It is through their reflection that the theme of barrenness is presented. *The London* in *The Living and the Dead* is also bereft of anything virtuous or joyful. Eliot himself feels and describes image of death refers image of skull which is a traditional emblem of death. Images of death haunt Elyot "swims in the confused sea that was anybody's London" (*LD*, 22).

The Waste Land echoes in "The Unreal City" which is re echoed in *The Living and the Dead*. The novel is "Eliot's Waste Land in extensor" (Burns 162). Bjorksten also associates Elyot, the principal character of *The Living and the Dead* with Eliot and *The Waste Land*, the sterile and dead. The genuine and artistic power of Eliot's poem must have influenced White and this paper proposes to make a study of the impact if Eliot's *The Waste Land* and White's *The Living and the Dead*.

Eliot and Patrick White both saw a complete breakdown of faith, culture and civilization in London. This city of broken faith was an "unreal city of shattered institutions, strained nerves and bankrupt ideals, where life no longer seemed serious or coherent," (Cox, *WL*, 101) and were people seemed already dead. The Waste Land is a picture of this modern world inhabited by those for whom life provides only a "heap of broken images" (*WL*, 1, 22) and "fear in a handful of dust" (*WL*, 30). Likewise *The Living and the Dead* demonstrates the metallic contemporary existence, were people are classified with two groups—the spiritually living and the living dead. The protagonist of both work, Tiresias and Elyot depict emotional and spiritual starvation–struggling to find meaning in meaningless universe. The long for a purpose of vitality that would redeem their "Dead Life" they refuse to leave their "Dead World" and discover solace in death. Tiresias makes no move to help the dead live again. Elyot also feels cut off from the family "It began to occupy him more and more, his not being part of anything...he stood a long way off and watched" (*LD*, 106). "He does not make use of opportunities to become alive, for him there is no rooted existence in the future or in his own mental make-up. His security is the past, a world of the dead" (Bjorksten, 33). He reflects on everything absent from the present "It was so easy to substitute the dead for the living, to build a cocoon of experience away from the noises in the street" (*LD*, 19). In *The Waste Land*, the first line "April is the cruellest month" (*WL*, 1) justifies that April, the month of pleasure is anticipated with fear which is linked with "memory and desire" (*WL*, 3), whereas Winter, the symbol of spiritual decay, maintains warmth. "Failure is not re-solved but it is demystified by being consciously explored. He surfaces from the fog and deadlines of retreat and thus what is implied is an awakening, from non-commitment, even if commitment is not achieve" (McCulloch, 313). The cyclic pattern is woven in *The Waste Land* with the use of fertility myths as decay and death are cyclical processes. In *The Living and the Dead* the circle is drawn by the three characters, Catherine, her daughter Eden, and her son Elyot, enclosed in a circle.

Tiresias the seer, reflects on the events of the past and present The Living in the Dead also depicts what lies latent in the space between the two moments. Elyot like Tiresias is the central consciousness, assimilating the characters together thus there is a unity imparted by the protagonist which achieved through the working of the conscious and unconscious psyche of different characters. Eliot uses images to depict the sordidness, and ugly soulless nature of contemporary existence.

A crowd flowed over London Bridge, so many,
I had not thought death had undone so many. (*WL*, 62-63)
Nothing can grow from this sterile land
What are the roots that clutch, what branches grow
Out of this stony rubbish. (*WL*, 20)

Same images "The sockets of his eyes were dark. Two empty saucers in the bone" (*LD*, 11).

Eliot speaks of "fear in a handful of dust" (*WL*, 30) while White likens Elyot's devotion to scholarship to a "devotion to dust." For Elyot, the emotion had gone out of his life, his life like his work was arranged in "numbered pages" (*LD*, 190) and he is a mere "rattler of bones." He is typical of the sterile man in the waste land, where the only noise heard is the "rattle of bones" (*WL*, 186).

Thus a comparative influence is "not confined to individual details or image or borrowings or even sources—it is something pervasive, something organically involved in and presented through artistic works" (Shaw, 91). Without any gainsaying it can be stated that *The Living and the Dead* not only echoes but implements images from *The Waste Land*. It also shares the overall atmosphere, "for all its skill and sureness in registering with fidelity, *The Living and the Dead* shows clear evidence of the author's reading of Eliot, not in the way of reference and quotation but rather of reading as influence on the sensibility" (Walsh, 7).

Works Cited

Bjorksten, Ingmar. *Patrick White—A General Introduction.* Queensland: University of Queensland Press, 1976. 33.

Burns, D.R. *The Directions of Australian Fiction 1920-74*. Melbourne: Casell Australia, 1975. 162.

Cox, (ed.). *T.S. Eliot*: *The Waste Land*. London: Penguin, 1968. 101.

Eliot, T.S. *The Man and His Work*. A, Tate Pelican. 36-37.

——. *The Waste Land*. 1, 22. Web.

McCulloch, Ann. "Patrick White's Novels and Nietzsche." *Australian Literature Studies*, Vol. 9, No. 2 (May 1980). 313.

Morely, Patricia. *The Mystery of Unity*. London: McGill-Green's University Press, 1972. 1.

Shaw, T.J. "Literary Indebtedness and Comparative Literary Studies," ed. Stallknect and Frenz, *Comparative Literature—Method and Perspective*. U.S.A.: Southern Illinois University Press, 1961. 91.

Walsh, William. *Patrick White's Fiction*. Australia: George Allen and Unwin, 1977. 7.

White, Patrick. *The Living and the Dead*. London: Macmillan, 1968. 101.

——. *The Living and the Dead*. London: Penguin, 1941. 106.

9

Emergence of Laura in Patrick White's *Voss*

Arun Kumar Yadav

The full name of Patrick White is Patrick Victor Martindale White. He is a British born Australian author. He is famous for novel, play, short fiction, poetry, autobiography and speeches. Name of some of his novels are as; *Happy Valley* (1939), *The Living and the Dead* (1941), *The Aunt's Story* (1948), *The Tree of Man* (1955), *Voss* (1957), *Riders in the Chariot* (1961), *The Solid Mandala* (1966), *The Vivisector* (1970), *The Eye of the Storm* (1973), *A Fringe of Leaves* (1976), *The Twyborn Affair* (1979), *Memoirs of Many in One* (1986) and *The Hanging Garden* (2012) (Unfinished). Some of his short story collections are *The Burnt Ones* (1964), *The Cockatoos* (1974), *Three Uneasy Pieces* (1987), etc. He won the Nobel Prize for Literature in 1973.

Patrick White's fifth novel *Voss* is arguably the highest achievement in the middle phase of his career. The book has now been translated into fifteen languages. Through his work White has firmly established his reputation in Australia as well as overseas. White's novels are mostly the complex explorations of isolation. In his novels, he often features unreliable and eccentric characters. His stories cover mostly Australian life. Although White's fiction deal with universal questions of human limitation and transcendence, it is grounded in the specifics of his own experience of time and place. Its politics are rooted in the greatness of the personal.

Voss is a historical novel in the Western tradition, showing a process through which a country achieves political independence. It is a complex and difficult novel. It seeks an attempt to reveal that it does work as a unified whole. Because, in a sense, it is a novel about diversity: those differences in human needs and aspirations. It is said that the protagonist of Voss is modelled on Ludwig Leichhardt, a German explorer who disappeared while attempting to cross the interior of the Australian continent during the 1840s. Contrasting the experience of outsiders in Australian society with those of the well-established middle class, much of the narrative alternates between Voss's journey across the outback, and the daily life of Laura Trevelyan, a young woman living in Sydney. Critics have interpreted Voss's journey as a metaphor for human suffering as well as a symbolic exploration of the Australian interior.

The present paper aims to clarify that *Voss* is partly an endeavour to rediscover the position of woman in Australian colonial history, which has been predominantly told and written from a masculine point of view. One may point out that the narrative of the voyage phase excludes female existence except, dream communion between Voss and Laura. That's why here is an attempt mostly to tackle the story which are related to women of the novel. However, there is also an attempt to show Laura's role throughout the text not as secondary, but primary at all. In fact, she is the one who sets the goal of Voss's journey. Furthermore, her metaphysical theory manipulates the reader's understanding of Voss's voyage. *Voss* also bears the mark of several other literary models. It continues the tradition of the 19th century English novel, because, its action begins in 1845 and ends in 1870. Not only is its action contained within the Victorian period but also represents a middle-class society, its social structures, and its manners, in a comic tone.

Around the narrative of the voyage, the relationship of Voss and Laura Trevelyn is woven. The second part shows the voyage entering the innermost deserts of Australia, facing extreme physical suffering, decay, death, mutiny and ultimate annihilation at the hands of the natives. With its stark and solid backdrops of visual colours, of startling exposure to the savagely primitive, there comes a rejection of time, which is almost always playful, and the need to clear oneself a space. Side by side is developed the psychic relationship of Voss and Laura through dreams and letters. The third part, covering several years after the rest, serves as an epilogue where Laura and Judd, the only survivor of the voyage, offers tribute to Voss.

The novel begins with Laura Trevelyan receiving an unaccustomed visit from a stranger, who turns out to be Voss. He reaches on a Sunday morning in the house of Mr. Bonner, who is a successful Sydney merchant and a primary sponsor of Voss's voyage. Laura was alone at that time, in the home. The full name of Voss is Johann Ulrich Voss who decides, arbitrarily, to lead a journey with half a dozen untrained men into the unexplored heart of nineteenth century Australia. The journey is only weeks away from departing when Voss finds himself strangely fallen in love to an unmarried English woman named Laura Trevelyan, who is an orphan and lives with her prosperous merchant uncle. Being in love of Laura, Voss sends a letter to her. His letter reaches to Laura, but, she struggles at first and thinks what to make of his unexpected proposal. She hardly knew this German fellow, and also she has a negative feeling about him. She also thinks that he despises her. Nevertheless, she could not ignore the proposal and finds herself agreeing to marry him.

But on the occasion of a party, organized by the Bonners, to celebrate the enterprise and departure of the expedition, Laura and Voss shed their modesty in the garden and passionately dispute on the issue of faith. It is the modesty between them that determines the course of their relationship. The garden, which is a border of the public and the personal, is also a place of introduction for White's female protagonists. Laura claims that her sense, which she believes is a superior faculty of women, enables her to enter into the minds of the most men. Thus, they part from each other. But after separating with each other they are not satisfied at all. Laura recovers her faith and love through pitying him. They are thus complementary to each other. Voss needs Laura to settle his ego, whereas Laura needs Voss to recover her faith. The goal of Voss's journey is fixed by Laura prior to his departure, that is, to achieve humility. However, in spite of her noticeable humility, the authorial voice implies Laura's instinct to control the man with an irony. Voss begins his journey to explore the Island. He promises her to write letters.

From that moment on, even though the harsh realities of Voss's voyage make it impossible for him to communicate with Laura again, their lives become inextricably linked in a way that goes beyond ordinary human affection and even, at times, that of ordinary human emotion. If Voss represents the modern Western ego, Laura's position in her advanced family deeply reminds the reader of the adoptive position of colonial Australia in its relation to Britain. It is immediately clear from this opening that Laura and Voss share otherness in common. In the course of their conversation, she attempts to cover her unknown fear of the Australian continent about which she has little understanding. Laura wears the mask of a passive woman and tries to flatter Voss's masculine pride. They love each other. Voss is clearly regarded as a stranger by Sydney residents who are mostly of British descent. The unknown fear of Laura about the continent shows that not only Voss, but also Laura is an explorer, struggling to establish her psychological and physical position in the adopted country. Laura projects her inner self upon Voss, which is symbolised by the motif of a mirror. In the opening scene, she looks into a glass hung in the living room while waiting for the visitor.

Focusing on Laura, it becomes clear that *Voss* is essentially a narrative of woman's independence, where a female protagonist struggles to win spiritual and physical independence from a patriarchal family. Laura at first appears as a self-sufficient but superficial lady who is submissive to her materialistic foster uncle. Then, she manages to depart Bonner's world of clear safety through her spiritual. Voss encourages her to face her true self with his persistent search for the infinite, and eventually achieves economic independence as a school teacher, the headmistress.

Furthermore, the writer depicts Laura as the same arrogant woman in the post-voyage part of the narrative, which makes it hard for the reader to sympathise with her. Recognising the omen of self-destruction in his pride, part of which she shares, Laura recovers her faith and love through pitying him. They are thus complementary to each other: Voss needs Laura to appease his ego, whereas Laura needs Voss to recover her faith. The goal of Voss's journey is fixed by Laura prior to his departure, that is, to achieve humility. Laura is aware of Voss's well-being, while Voss recognises her shadow in landscapes and sees her in dreams which recur throughout the journey.

The novel explores the nature and meaning of love on many different levels—love between an eccentric man and an equally eccentric woman, love between a leader and the otherwise mismatched travelling companions whom fate and his own uncontrolled egotism have bound together in mutual adversity, the love a human being may or may not feel for God even as he or she resents His omnipotence and seeks in vain for concrete proof of His existence.

When the novel opens, Rose as the housemaid introduces and attends to Voss and Laura, the description emphasising her as an important symbolic intermediary in their relationship. On a symbolic level, Voss and Laura are drawn to each other because of their corporeality and sexuality, which Rose represents. Physical attraction will remain for the most part unacknowledged, until Laura eventually absorbs Rose's associations, but a strong seam of barely repressed sexual energy defines their relationship from the start. Laura denies and projects her yearnings, with the consequence that the bodies of servants are discomfortingly sexual. Rose's sexuality and corporeality is extended into the image of the rose itself as symbolic associations, typically in White's fiction, expand via word association, metaphor and metonymy. The progress of Laura and Voss's relationship is tracked by the transformation roses undergo in the Bonners' garden.

Yet initially Laura is as defined by a defensive abjection as her rational counterpart, Voss. This similarity is important because Laura's eventual acceptance of corporeality allows her to become Voss's mystical preceptor and extends his self-enclosed character the possibility of a redemptive openness to others and otherness. Rose is presented as heavily personified, Laura's body remains obscured, firstly by the dimness of the room, secondly by the description of her clothing, which is itself barely visible in the gloom, and thirdly by the perpetually ambivalent narrative treatment that contributes to her mysterious nature.

Voss is also a remarkably vivid examination of the mindset of colonial Australia—a place where true men of vision were in remarkably short supply but were not always welcomed or embraced when they appeared. Laura's struggles to gain the acceptance and respect of her acquaintances and her strait-laced aunt and uncle, to overcome the restrictions placed on women by rigid codes of behaviour. Laura waits in Sydney, syntactically reinventing the resistant trace of space or time. When Voss and Laura are not together, the relationship takes place in the mind, with some sort of sixth sense resulting in a synchronisation of feelings. Their love blossoms across time, transcending the barriers of a class driven society. Voss proposes in a letter, and Laura waits for him. It is a heartbreaking romance, the two strong-willed individuals, both outsiders, binding their fates together. An unlikely romance, it is haunting and touching. To add to its scope Laura also gets a child, sweet Mercy, in one of White's elegant plot twists.

As this description suggests, the body is not so easily dismissed or suppressed. Laura must overcome her loathing to her inherent animality to accept her love for Voss, an overcoming symbolised in her increasing affection for Rose. Voss too will find that physical loathing precludes the experience of love. He is to some degree aware that his rejection of the physical is to his own harm, and although he awkwardly continues to disclaim it, he longs for the human companionship that he associates with materiality.

The text depicts the aftermath of Voss's death in the remaining three sections. Towards the end, Laura, now a headmistress speaks about the meaning of Voss's journey at a party to the select members of Sydney society who are willing to explore the unknown territory of their mind. While Voss is away in the desert, Bonner's maid, Rose, gives birth to an illegitimate child. Laura names the girl, Mercy, and adopts her after the Rose's death by childbirth. Dutton and Tacey regard Mercy as an unnecessary appendix to the Voss and Laura relationship.

Voss's journey toward the acceptance of corporeality cannot be detached from Laura's, and the latter is unable to dispense with flesh in its embodiment as Rose Portion. Although she tries to be kind to Rose, Laura initially shies from the slightest physical communication that elicits a response from the servant. Their interaction is thus greatly inhibited, and Laura is incapable of expressing compassion. It is only with special effort that she is able to smile at Rose, because Rose's response is immediate and repellent. Laura therefore finds herself in a bind, unable to escape her feelings of disgust. This is a central tension for the character, whose responses are, as we have seen, contradictory. The ambiguity evident here is again important to an understanding of Laura's transformation from egoist rationalist to humble saint. She is disgusted and unhappy because Rose, as maidservant, brushes her hair and hence literally touches her; as the latter, her disgust is the source of unhappiness because Rose's breasts touch her, that is, it evokes her thought.

Physical attraction will remain for the most part unacknowledged, until Laura eventually absorbs Rose's associations, but a strong seam of barely repressed sexual energy defines their relationship from the start. Laura denies and projects her yearnings, with the consequence that the bodies of servants are discomfortingly sexual. The lurking presence and leisurely sexuality of Jack Slipper, the father of Rose's child, is deeply disturbing to Laura until his departure from the Bonners' property, provoked by his arrest for drunkenness. Jack, however, leaves behind him the pregnant Rose, a body continuing to disturb and repel because it awakens Laura's attention to sexuality and becomes associated with her disgust for her own developing physical attraction to Voss.

Rose Portion symbolises animality, corporeality and sexuality in the novel, aspects of existence disclaimed but eventually embraced by Laura Trevelyan who thereafter becomes associated with the abject, her arising in Voss's visions to test his self-sufficiency and to threaten the borders of his subjectivity. Laura's appearances to Voss suggest that he should embrace humility in the face of the unbelievable alterity beyond the limits of his consciousness. An alterity seemingly incorporating the physical world, corporeality, notions of the feminine, unknowable regions of the self, and an overwhelming sense of the unrepresentable sacred.

In White, it is an understanding of the whole process of time, which is basically the timeless, to be free of the memory of time that is radically not in keeping with that of discursive meaning. It leads to a specific cultural identity—a theme that is central to the novel's design and further there is the weaving of the web that integrates several cultures, and anchors it in the geography of the land, its sands, deserts, scrubs, rocks and dead trees, and in the lives of the different inhabitants of the land, the aboriginal tribes, convicts, ex-convicts, immigrants, and the offspring of the originally English families born on the Australian continent.

Voss is also about Australia and its national identity, combining an English strain, a German strain, and an aboriginal strain, weaving all these yarns together. White's writing achieves, as in his other novels, an Australian text of extraordinary depth and proportions, which conveys and contains a multiple cultural identity. There are several questions being raised. Does life transcend time? Is time a dimension of the eternal, which can transform the past as well as the present, changing and re-ordering the artistic heritage? Mysticism and corporeality are intimately related in White's fiction and that a communion with God, according to White, correlates with the apprehension of physicality. The ritual of communion is an important thematic focus of White's writing, enacting the incorporation of corporeality into the self.

Works Cited

Barua, Krishna. "The Cosmic and Acosmic—A Redefinition of Being and Time in Patrick White's *Voss*." *IRWLE* VI. II (July 2010): 1-5.

Brandy, Veronica. "In My End Is My Beginning: Laura as Heroine of Voss." *Southerly*, 35.1 (1975): 16-32.

Tacey, David J. *Patrick White: Fiction and the Unconscious*. Melbourne: Oxford University Press, 1988.

White, Patrick. *Voss*. London: Penguin, 2008.

10

The Fourth World Shouts Back... "We Have Arrived"

Neha Arora

Ngugiwa Thiongo, in his *Barrel of a Pen: Resistance to Repression in Neo-Colonial Kenya* asserted the power of 'pen' in reversing the centre-margin relationship between the colonizer and colonized. However, literature, be of any region, cannot be studied in isolation; the socio-cultural-political surroundings that go into its making lend completeness to its meaning. The ethnicities, the roots, the origins, all are the chief ingredients of any literary work and to reach out to this bedrock, the native people are the best resources. The indigenous people of Canada, U.S.A., Australia (Aborigines), New Zealand (Maories), Finland (Laplanders), etc. are clubbed less than one umbrella term, the Fourth World, coined by George Manuel and Michael Posluns in their book, *The Fourth Way: An Indian Reality* in 1974. Suffering centuries of suppression and exclusion, these natives have finally found their voice in the moves taken in the second half of the last century to assimilate them in the mainstream. The geographical barriers separating the minorities across the world have been dismantled by the numerous measures taken to voice the devoiced, one such being the creation of the World Council of Indigenous People (WCIP) in 1975. The society was sanctioned the status of an NGO by the United Nations. It was at the inaugural meeting of WCIP that George Manuel introduced the concept of the Fourth World, to describe the "indigenous minorities throughout the earth" (*Black Words, White Page*, Adam Shoemaker, 1).

The present paper undertakes the origin and purpose of Aboriginal literature in Australia, primarily focusing on the genre of poetry. Although many poets have exploited the Aboriginal myths and in turn, preserved their culture (that was under threat) in their writings, I shall be confining myself only to the pioneers of Aboriginal poetry. Established first as a penal colony, Australia gradually became the 'all Whites land' (read British), marginalising the indigenous people, the Aborigines. Ashcroft et al. use the term for the indigenous peoples born in a place or region:

> The term 'aboriginal' was coined as early as 1667 to describe the indigenous inhabitants of places encountered by European explorers, adventurers or seamen. While the term 'aboriginal' and 'aborigine' have been used from time to time to describe the indigenous inhabitants of many settler colonies, they are now most frequently used as a shortened form of 'Australian Aborigine' to describe the indigenous inhabitants of Australia. (2009: 4)

The owners were treated with such brutality that their number dwindled from 300,000 in 1788 to merely 60,000 in 1930. This data was an alarm for the think tanks of both the communities and immediate efforts were required to set the wrong things right. In geographical terms, Australia is the smallest continent of the world but at the same time, it is the largest island too. In the present, it comprises the Australian mainland, Tasmania and several other islands, together called the Commonwealth of Australia. It was post Captain James Cook's invasion in 1788 that the penal colony of New South Wales was established. Later other colonies of the British empire such as Tasmania (1825), Western Australia (1829), South Australia (1836), Victoria (1851) and Queensland (1859) were added and in 1901 they came together to form what is today known as the Commonwealth of Australia. A brief history of Australia informs us that the land projected as *terra nullius* to the world was actually inhabited by the indigenous people even before the British unfurled their flag on 'Aboriginaland'. But with the coming of the Whites, the natives were eliminated, either by coercion or by the irrational policies of the government such as the Protection Acts, the Commonwealth of Australia Constitution Act 1900, the Assimilation Policy, the White Australian Policy, etc. Such policies exerted great impact in dividing the population, so much so that the native people were not counted in the census. It was only in 1967 that they have got the citizenship rights. The Aborigines suffered "not only economically, but politically, judicially, socially, and culturally, Black Australian suffered at the hands of white politicians, policy-makers, and pastoralists" (Shoemaker, 17). The various policies to maintain the segregation were diligently implemented by the Whites government.

The twentieth century awakened the Aborigines to the shocking reality and they became increasingly assertive for their rights. Realizing the strengths in their roots, they revived the Aboriginal culture that was fundamental to define them and eventually reinvigorated Australian literature by contributing a lot in every genre. They themselves started agitation for their representation and the world received them with open arms indicating "the growing confidence and fluency of Aborigines operating within the constraints of White Australian culture" (Shoemaker, 3). The resistance came in all the spheres: social, political, even literature. It is indeed commendable that whereas in 1961 no Black Australian had published any creative work, by 1988 some twelve plays, eighteen poetry collections and seven novels had already come! The Aboriginal literature developed not as an off-shoot but parallel to Australian (mainstream) literature. It privileged the readers' world over to see the Aborigines through their lens and not that of the Europeans, as was the case until then. It introduced the readers a world of traumas, of differences, and also the need to overcome those differences. The indigenous talent that was hitherto unknown to the world was discovered. The appearance of Oodgeroo Noonuccal's (Kath Walker) first collection of poetry *We Are Going* in 1964 ushered a new era of "self-reflective literary examination by Black Australians" (Shoemaker, 5).

Simultaneously, the socio-political scene was also changing. The Aboriginal resistance movements date back to the 1920s, coming to full bloom in 1960s. The Australian Aborigines Progressive Association (1924-27), the Euralian Association of Western Australia (1934), the Aboriginal petition to the King (1937), the William Fergusan's Aborigines' Progressive Association (APA, 1934) and finally the Federal Council for the Advancement of Aboriginal and Torres Strait Islanders (FCAATSI) were working significantly in the 1960s and in 1961, Aborigines were finally granted franchise throughout Australia. Both, the socio-political and literary world co-operated in the overhaul of the society and the amelioration of the Aborigines.

The Australian Aboriginal writing got more confidence with its inclusion in the purview of Australian literature. With the popularity of Kath Walker, Jack Davis, Kevin Gilbert, Colin Johnson, Ruby Langford, Sally Morgan, etc., Aboriginal writers declared their arrival on the mainstream. The leitmotif of their writing is to vindicate their existence, to reclaim the lost rights and dignity, and to re-write their history, hitherto concealed from the world. All writing was to instil in the Aboriginals concern for their land that had been usurped by the Whites. Josie Douglas and Marg Bowman also focus on the Aboriginal poetry used as political manifesto:

> Aboriginal people were writing in a time of great political change and activism, land rights and the right to vote were all part of this era. Poetry at this time carried the voice of protest and was used as a political tool. Aboriginal poetry today still carries a political message...Black poetry is a commentary on Black lives, showing the diversity and range of the Aboriginal experience. ("Indigenous Culture", 35)

The social, political and personal elements are all intertwined and can be unanimously felt in all the writers. Jindyworobak movement, founded in 1938 in Adelaide by the poet Rex Ingamells was a nationalist movement to protect the indigenous culture from the alien effects. Primarily a literary movement, the writers aimed at projecting Australia from the Australian/native's perspective and not from that of the European. Aboriginal literature emerged from Aboriginal sufferings and hence, in the entire corpus, politics, life and literature go together. The writers celebrate the bush life and harmony with nature, at the same time, memories of massacre and violence dominate their literature. Cliff Watego elaborates upon the need of discussing the socio-cultural-political position of the 'dispossessed and diasporic aborigines' by quoting Jack Davis:

> We used to speak in those days when we were talking about politics—black politics—of how we were going to make ourselves heard within the white Australian society. And even in those days when we went back to our little dingy rooms, we said (referring to, among others, Kath Walker, Faith Bandler, and Ken Colbung), 'well we've got to write about this, we've got to tell the people.' ("Backgrounds to Australian Literature", 11)

A distinct literature was established with the aim for a pan-Aboriginality. Bruce McGuinness advised that the

> Aboriginal writers have responsibility here, a very important responsibility, to take that message not only to white people but to Aboriginal people as well, so that we can foster within our own communities a very important concept. That concept is that we are going to survive, we are going to have to do it as a community, we are going to have to do it as a nation and not as individuals. ("The Politics of Aboriginal Literature", 46-47)

Like other indigenous writings across the world, Aboriginal literature too emphasized not to be defined and judged by the outsiders. In an attempt to correct the negative image created by the Whites and also to articulate their anger, the Aboriginal writers violated the standards of English language. Alexis Wright argues that in their literature, the writers 'challenge(s) the non-Aboriginal perceptions of standard English' with their different linguistic expressions. Anita Heiss chooses to call it 'Aboriginalisation' of English language or to use Kenny Laugton's phrase, the 'Blackfella lingo'. Drawing much from the oral traditions was a favourite with the writers to cement their faith in the firm roots of their culture. Jennie Bell asserts that

Aboriginal writing give an opportunity to realize their identity: "This is who I am and I'm proud of who I am" (Heiss, 41) and hence it is important to retain the aboriginality in their writing.

In sync with the other literatures of the subalterns across the world, Aboriginal literature too had a two-pronged strategy—to destroy and to re-create; to demolish the wrong notions about the natives as perpetrated by the Whites, and also to re-write their history from their own perspective. It functions as an eye-opener to the non-Aboriginals. Mudrooroo Narogin opined, "Aboriginal literature begins as a cry from the heart directed at the White man. It is a cry for justice and for a better deal, a cry for understanding and an asking to be understood" (*Writing From the Fringe*, 1). His Holiness Pope John Paul II at the meeting with Aboriginal and Torres Strait Islander people at Alice Springs on 20 November 1986 congratulated the Aborigines for their regaining of the voice and at the same time also motivated them:

> You have kept your sense of brotherhood. If you stay closely united, you are like a tree standing in the middle of a bush-fire sweeping through the timber. The leaves are scorched and the tough bark is scarred and burned; but inside the tree the sap is still flowing, and under the ground the roots are still strong. Like that tree you have endured the flames, and you still have the power to be reborn. The time for this rebirth is now!

Commendable work began to be done in exposing the wealth of knowledge of the Australian past; in this context, one can recall two major works of the noted historian Henry Reynolds, *Aborigines and Settlers* and *The Other Side of the Frontier*. With such works, Aboriginals began to be recognized in the world and became what W.E.H. Stanner puts, little more than 'a melancholy footnote' (*After the Dreaming*, 25). The near invisibility of the Aborigines was over and David Unaipan, with his *Native Legends* (1929) emerged as the first Black Australian writer in English.

Aboriginal Australian verse proper begins with Kath Walker (later Oodgeroo Noonuccal—1920-93). She was the 'people's poet' who set a promising example for Aboriginal literature with her two poetry collections, *We Are Going* (1964) and *The Dawn is at Hand* (1966). Adam Shoemaker calls her 'the doyenne of Aboriginal writers' (181). Her excessive political involvement for the rights of the Black Australians gave impetus to her poetry. She was a key figure in reforming the Australian constitution and spearheaded many movements to include the Aborigines as the legal citizens of Australia. In her role as a literary artist, her political activism gets blended. Herself a teacher-educator, she established the Noonuccal-Nughie Education and Cultural Centre at her private property in Moongalba where she taught Aboriginal culture to all the children, irrespective of their colour. Born as Kathlean Jean Mary Ruska, known as Kath Walker, she changed her name to Oodgeroo Noonuccal in 1988. Her childhood was spent in utter poverty serving as domestic maid to many White Australian families. However her poetry took every one in sway, enthralling with its lucid style blended with the protest element. Initially her poetry was rejected by the critics as 'not conforming to the permissible norms' (set by the white writers), its crude and harsh vocabulary and style shocked the sophisticated readers and critics. She was adamant to reclaim the lost dignity of the Aborigines and to shake both the communities. Her poetry expresses concern over the drastic transition that has taken place in Australia, socially, culturally and politically. Giving a contrasting picture of the past and present in her poem "Then and Now" (*My People*) she writes:

> No more woomera, no more boomerang,
> No more the play about, no more the old ways.
> Children of nature we were then,
> No clocks hurrying crowds to toil.
> Now I am civilized and work in the white way,
> Now I have a dress, now I have shoes:
> 'Isn't she lucky to have a good job!'
> Better when I had only a dillybag.
> Better when I had nothing but happiness.

The rustic, carefree life of the past has been thrown to the wind; the identity markers, 'woomera', 'boomerang' have been forgotten behind the façade of sophistication but what is 'achieved' cannot compensate for what is 'lost'. She further points at the loss and erosion of the native culture:

> We belong here, we are of the old ways.
> We are the corroboree and the bora ground,
> ....
> The scrubs are gone, the hunting and the laughter.
> The eagle is gone, the emu and the kangaroo are gone from this place.
> The bora ring is gone.
> The corroboree is gone.
> And we are going. ("We are Going")

Although the damage done by the Whites is irrevocable but the history lives on; the past cannot be eradicated and this past is the propelling factor in their struggle against the invaders. The myths, the ceremonies, the rituals are deeply ingrained in the psyche of the natives that can never be erased by the foreign culture:

> Let no one say the past is dead.
> The past is all about us and within.
> Haunted by tribal memories, I know
> This little now, this accidental present
> Is not the all of me, whose long making
> Is so much of the past.... ("The Past")

Anne Brewster observes that "for Aboriginal people the narration of the past has the additional role of producing a sense of unity and group solidarity. The awareness of a common past can thus bind together people who have been dispossessed" (*Aboriginality and Sally Morgan's 'My Place'*, 53-54). Noonuccal's contribution lies in introducing an Aboriginal perspective in the so-called 'Australian literary canon'. She emphasizes: "I see my books as the voice of the Aboriginal people, not my own personal voice. They dictate what I write" (quoted in Shoemaker, 186). She pioneered the group of poets that was later to be joined by Kevin Gilbert, Jack

Davis and the likes. Her poetry "celebrated aboriginal survival in the face of adversity, lamented prejudice and oppression, and offered an optimistic view of the potential for interracial harmony in the country" (186). Labelled as 'propaganda' by the critics, Noonuccal nevertheless continued composing verses to instil pride in the natives as well as to condemn the irrational policies of the Whites. Expressing her concern over the mining operations, she wrote:

> The miner rapes
> The heart of earth
> With his violent spade
> Stealing, bottling her black blood
> For the sake of greedy trade. ("Time is Running Out")

She laments on the passing away of the Aboriginal culture yet maintains the faith that the natives could not be eradicated. They are the rooted people although the roots are weakening; tone of dispossession coincides with that of hope of resurrection. She also drafted the famous 'Aboriginal Charter of Rights' presented at the 5th Annual General Meeting of the Federal Council for the Advancement of Aborigines and Torres Strait Islanders, held in Adelaide in 1962, demanding:

> Make us neighbours, not fringe-dwellers;
> Make us mates, not poor relations,
> Citizens, not serfs on stations.
> Must we native old Australians
> In our own land rank as aliens?
> Banish ban and conquer caste,
> Then we'll win our own at last.

The celebration of Aboriginality further gained momentum with Kevin Gilbert's (1933-93) *End of Dreamtime* (1971). He opines: "White people's devaluation of Aboriginal life, religion, culture and personality caused the thinking about self and race that I believe is the key to modern Aboriginal thinking" (*Living Black*, 2). Unlike the fellow writers, Gilbert moves a step ahead. Adopting a very practical and rational approach and using direct, often crude language, he introspects into the lacunae of his own race. Although the Whites have damaged their lives to the extent of irreparability, the crevices within the community could not be overlooked. As the 'petty bourgeoisie' of Africa, in Australia too were the 'better blacks' who had turned traitors to their motherland and fellow brethren. In his poem "Better Blacks" he lashes out to such neo-colonialist:

> Watched for the traitors
> Dressed in black
> Watch for those jackies
> Up you Jack!
> Watch for the puppet
> Watch for the brute
> Living like a Whiteman
> Grey serge suit. (*People are Legends*, 26-27)

In compliance with the Aboriginal writing, Gilbert admits to have "adopted writing as means of voicing the Aboriginal situation...I try to present as truly as possible the Aboriginal situation and the Aboriginal response" (Personal Interview in May 1981, Canberra). At the same time he proposes very realistically that until the White Australians understand and acknowledge the Blacks, no amount of struggle would really benefit.

He was the son of an English/Irish father and a half-caste mother, and his mixed parentage was the origin of his investigation into the complex relationship between these two races. He took up the same theme in his poem "Inhabitants of the Third World":

> But when the day came and shadows departed
> I found I was a world apart.
> Soon they whispered to me no more,
> Said I was different. Only the bravest
> Came to my shelter at night. I stood apart
> From the kinsfolk of my mother.
> I left the campfire, turned towards the city,
> Condemned by the blood of my father.... (*End of Dreamtime*, 9-10)

Gilbert represented the miserable condition of the half-castes who were not accepted by either of the communities and treated with scepticism. He introduces to the readers a very significant issue of Australian Policy of 'Stolen Generations', which was projected by the White government as a welfare policy but was actually the policy of 'gentle genocide'. Stolen Generations (this term was coined by the historian Peter Read in 1982 in his report written for the New South Wales government) is a euphemistic phrase for the 'half-caste' children who were 'legally' (forcibly) separated from their mothers in the name of educating them.

'Land' was yet another major theme with Gilbert, as was with other writers. Land is their identity and the aboriginals shared an inextricable relationship with it. "No discussion about Aboriginal affairs can take place without first establishing the fundamentals: land and compensation as a point of justice. To give black people in all states a sense of belonging once again; the restoration of a land base that affirms that the people have a place, a value in this country...such things are at the heart of a solution to the ills of Aboriginal Australia" (quoted in 'Kevin Gilbert and *Living Black*', 8). Landscape was/is never seen as a piece of land by the aboriginal writers, it is a storehouse of their spiritual and religious beliefs. The natives experience a kind of mystical union with the land and their ancestors. They celebrate their rivers, their hills, their forests in their writing. Even Ronald Paul Hill corroborates that the Aborigines looked at land as something "as a part of themselves, and they are part of that—the land. The land and they are one." ("Blackfellas and Whitefellas: Aboriginal Land Rights, The Mabo Decision, and the Meaning of the Land", 303-22).

In his poem "Aboriginal Query", Gilbert vents out his anger in a very subtle manner:

What do you want
Whiteman?
What do you need from me?
You have taken my life
My culture
My dreams

You have leached the substance
Of love from my being
You have leached the substance
Of race from my loins
Why do you persist?...
What do you seek?
Why do you destroy me
Whiteman?
Why do you destroy that
Which you cannot hope to understand.... (*People are Legends*, 48)

The Whites had always devalued what was Aboriginal and have targeted their confidence in themselves. The Aboriginal culture is far beyond their comprehension, despite this they did meddle in their affairs. In his poems "The Gurundji", "Look, Koori", etc. he coaxes his people to come together and realize the richness of their culture:

Die as a man if die you must
Die as a man born free
It's better to die than to live a life
As gutless scum, Koori. (*People are Legends*, 52)

He encouraged his people to fight against injustice. Besides poetry, he also wrote a play "The Cherry Orchard" while in jail for killing his wife. The play is the first to be written in English by an Aboriginal. It was awarded the Captain Cook Memorial Award and became a symbol of protest of the Aboriginals in 1988 against the Bicentennial celebration of the European empire. In the same year, he was awarded the Human Rights and Equal Opportunity Commissions' Human Rights Award for Literature (which he later returned) for the anthology of Aboriginal poetry he edited, *Inside Black Australia*. For his *Living Black: Blacks talk to Kevin Gilbert* (1977), he was awarded the National Book Council Award in 1978. He also wrote another anthology of Aboriginal poetry in 1978, *People are Legends*. Like Noonuccal, he too was much active for the rights of his fellow Aborigines.

To quote his words, "(My art) exhibitions (in the late 60s and 70s) confirmed my resolve to use my poems, writing and art to open up to the question of the continuing denial of an injustice against Aboriginals, in an effort to bring the reality of the white Australian inhumanity onto the open."

Jack Davis too enforces the relationship between the mother(land) and the son in his poem "Yadabooka":

> The desert wind, the harsh sun, your tribal land
> Is part of you, your very soul.
> How can a stranger understand? (*The First Born and Other Poems*, 21)

Here, the 'stranger' is very clearly the Whites who can never identify with the land. Jack Davis's contribution to Aboriginal writing is immense. With his *The First Born and Other Poems* (1970), followed by *Jagardoo* (1978), "Kullark" (1979), "The Dreamers" (1981), "No Sugar" (1986) and "Barungi" (1989) to name a few, he emphasized that to keep oneself in existence, the Aboriginal need to remain uncontaminated by the European culture. He strongly was against the tendency of camouflaging by the natives. While describing the 'massacre' (physical and psychological) done by the colonizers in his poem "Aboriginal Australia", he sounds like Bostock's "Black Children". The words may be different but the essence, the angst is the same.

> To the Others
> You once smiled a friendly smile,
> Said we were kin to one another,
> Thus with guile for a short while
> Became to me a brother.
> Then you swamped my way of gladness,
> Took my children from my side,
> Snapped shut the law book,
> ...
> And I wondered when I would find a pen
> To prove your freckled mind.
> ...You murdered me with rope, with gun

The massacre of my enclave,
...Now you primly say you're justified,
And sing of a nation's glory,
But I think of a people crucifies—
The real Australian story.

Gerry Bostock very sarcastically he exposes how the intruders came and divided the natives. In his poem, "Black Children", he delineates the strategy adopted by the Whites initially to settle down in Australia. Under the pretext of creating a prosperous nation, they erased the centuries—long civilization and culture:

The white man settled this vast country;
Cleared the land;
Built a great nation democratic and free,
And they looked after you, their friends,
Our brothers, the Aborigine. (17)

Like 'Judas', they feigned friendship and made false promises of 'protecting' the Aborigines, else the latter 'would have dies of disease/ or starved if they left you to roam....' But by pouring acid in the roots, they have succeeded in collapsing the giant tree and now enjoy as the natives 'grovelled for fresh air/ Under his racist care;/ Derelict and abused.' Thus, now the true Australian story is told to the world, the brutalities of the whites are now revealed. However, witnessing the confidence and determination in the protests of the Aboriginals, the Whites now expect them to move on and start afresh, without any malice against the invaders. Jack Davis caustically remarks that how can the Aborigines be asked to forgive and forget the past, when the White Australians cannot forget what happened to them in the past? Kevin Gilbert, echoing the same thought, asks these White people: "...cut off a man's leg, kill his mother, rape his land, psychologically attack and keep him in a powerless position each day—does it not live on in the mind of the victim? Does it not continue to scar and affect the thinking? Deny it, but it still exists" (*Aboriginal Writing Today*, 41). The traumatic past and violent history forms the crux of their entire literature and therefore, can never be disremembered.

Australia and the natives now mourn of the loss of their culture, and also the sons of the soil. The invaders brought with them Books, Bibles, Schools and Churches, replacing the indigenous system and ultimately things fell apart. The culture, the education, the religion—all was White now. In his 'The First Born', Davis makes the motherland question in despair,

> Where are my first-born, said the brown land, sighing;
> They came out of my womb long, long ago.
> They were formed of my dust-why, why are they crying
> And the light of their being barely aglow?
> I strain my ears for the sound of their laughter.
> Where are the laws and the legends I gave?
> Tell me what happened, you whom I bore after.
> Now only their spirits dwell in the caves.
> You are silent, you cringe from replying.
> A question is there, like a blow on the face.
> The answer is there when I look at the dying,
> At the death and neglect of my dark proud race.

The writers were politically involved and reflected upon the social conditions of the time they lived in. Jack Davis rightly pointed out: "...most Aboriginal writers were involved within the Black movement.... We all started off as political people" ('An Interview with Jack Davis', 116). Hence their writing was not aloof of the social awareness; the literariness and message were well blended together. The feeling of resistance and protest could be easily felt. Like the other subaltern literatures across the world, the Aboriginal literature too did not believe in the dictum of 'art for art's sake', directly or indirectly their focus was to reinforce the 'identity' factor in the natives and to teach them to be proud of their identity. The following words from Davis' famous play 'The Dreamers' aptly foreground the state to which the Aboriginals were reduced: "You have turned our land into a desolate place. We stumble along with a half-white mind. Where are we? What are we? Not a recognised race. There is a desert ahead and a desert behind" (1989, 4-71). This justifies the bitterness and the anguish in their writings. Resistance, retaliation, assertion were needed to break the hegemony of the Whites. Aboriginal Literature aided in putting an end to the culture of silence and the strong whirlwind of this new literature did succeed in creating the desirous effects. Shoemaker draws from Shana Howard's song 'Solid Rock' that expresses a sense of guilt in the new-generation Whites for the wrongs done by their ancestors to the Black Australians:

They were standin' on the shore one day
Saw the white sails in the sun.
Wasn't long before they felt the sting
White man—White law—White gun
Don't tell me that it's justified
'Causc somewhere—
Someone lied.

And realizing this treachery and mindless abnegation of one's own culture, the poets continuously/rigorously instigate the natives to fight for their rights. Davis's 'Let Go' and Bostock's 'Black Children' are call for unity. Bostockinstigates the 'black children' to unite and revolt, to snatch their rights:

Prepare Black Children
For the Land Rights fight,
Our cause is true,
Our aim's in sight,
Unite my people
Unite!
Come on, Black Children
Rise on your feet!
Get out of the gutter
And onto the street;
United together,
Hand in hand,
Heads raised high we stand,
Then, march as one,
Surging forward and onward,

For justice
For freedom
And for our land! (*Black Man Coming*, 18)

Without much formal education, Bostock too, like other Aboriginal writers, had an impoverished childhood, taking up menial jobs for survival. In 1972, he initiated his career as 'reformist/revolutionist', getting involved in the struggle for Aboriginal rights in Canberra. He was active in the street theatre and also established the Black Theatre in Sydney. He also published 'Here Comes the Nigger', a play in 1974.

However, the writers experimented with other forms too yet poetry was seen as the best and most popular medium among all the genres available. Whether it was the popular *Bulletin* or a regional magazine like the *Stick* or *The Kimberly Land Council Newsletter*, the Black Australian poetry found its place as a regular feature. Drawing much from their ancestral tradition was a deliberate move by the poets. Shoemaker elaborates that, "Oodgeroo Noonuccal discovered this poetic door; Kevin Gilbert began to open it; but it is urban poets like Bobbi Sykes, Aileen Corpus and Lionel Fogarty who are beginning to cross the threshold" (215). This helped the writers two-way: firstly this was the world they personally knew and secondly, this was an attempt to re-establish their faith in their culture, as also make the Whites realize the richness and strength of the tradition they had trampled upon. It was necessary to reconstruct the past and rejuvenate the lost heritage. The Aboriginals were staunchly in opposition of the Assimilationist policy of the White government. They asserted their individuality. Maureen Watson writes to rectify the negative image with which Aboriginals are associated:

'Aboriginal and', yes, your birthright
No matter what some name it;
So dig your fingers deep in the soil,
And feel it, and hold it, and claim it.
Your people fought and died for this,
Tho' history books distort it all,

But in your veins runs that same Aboriginal blood,
So walk tall, my child, walk tall.... (*Black Reflections*, 15)

Felicitated with many national and international awards for her incessant contribution in the Aboriginal rights' struggle, she was one of the respected Aboriginal women. She was one of the founding members of various indigenous organizations such as the Radio Redfern and the Aboriginal People's gallery. Her first collection of poems and short stories, *Black Reflections* was published in 1982.

Such optimistic, enthusiastic writings imbued a great sense of confidence in the Aborigines. It heralded their presence on the social as well as literary scene. The Aborigines were now prepared to confront the Whites and rise like a rising sun.

Let go of my hand
Let me be what I want to be
Let go of my hand
The sands of time are trickling before me
I have not yet achieved
What I want to be
Let go of my hand
I want to stand alone
In a sea of words
Pluck out the phrases
Soar like a bird
I want to stand on a mountain
Wait for the dawn
Yet be aware of
The approaching storm
I want to fashion a rainbow
That arcs through the sky
And iron out the dilemmas
Between you and I. ("Let Go", Jack Davis)

Aboriginal writing, like the Dalit Literature in India, is never free of revolution. It was written with a purpose as is evident in the foregone discussion. Wilde et al. argue that Aboriginal writing has "never been divorced from the Aboriginal struggle for economic freedom, legal recognition and reform of basic living conditions...it asserts (that) literature is one of the ways of getting political things done" (Wilde, 17). The new wave of literature has opened new debates about the 'people on the fringes'. It signalled that the once marginalized, in society as well as in literature, are no more the subalterns. However, Aboriginal literature also reiterates the need of a complete reworking of the 'assimilationist policy' is sought after that would integrate the shut-outs. The racial segregation that was in practice until few decades ago was observed by Maureen Watson as a kind of apartheid with 'a white, intrusive majority and a black, original minority' but she asserts that 'it is time to hold black mirror for black reflections' (Shoemaker, 278). The black requires to see himself through his own eyes and realize the beauty in his blackness. In the view of Colin Jonson, writers should talk about the past, focus on present and think about future. They ought to be very conscious and alert about the subject matter along with the language they choose to write. He believes that 'Only Aborigines can really write about Aborigines.' Similar views are shared by Oodgeroo Noonuccal that "Only Aborigines can understand what is happening to themselves at this moment" (quoted in Shoemaker, 276). Although Aboriginal literature is a recent phenomenon, a great onus lied upon the writers who could bring about the necessary revolution and they did succeed, the need is to maintain the success. The initial writers, like torchbearers, paved the way for the renowned writers/names such as A.D. Hope, Judith Wright, Patrick White, their contribution is indeed incomparable. They re-instated the presence of Aborigines in the annals of history and celebrated Aboriginality in their writings. They re-represented the marginalised voices and re-directed the natives to their land, the large repository of social, moral, ethical values. They were the harbingers of a new dawn that announced the arrival of the Fourth World, and also their stay!!

Works Cited

Ashcroft et al. *Post-Colonial Studies: The Key Concepts*. London: Routledge, 2000, reprint in India 2009.

Bell, Jeanie. Quoted in 'Indigenous Discourse' in *To Talk Straight* by Anita Heiss. Aboriginal States Press. http://www.aiatsis.gov.au/aboriginal_studies_press/orderpp 41.

Bostock, Gerry. "Black Children", in *Black Man Coming*. Privately printed. Melbourne, 1980, 17.

Brewster, Anne. *Aboriginality and Sally Morgan's My Place*. South Melbourne: Sydney University Press, 1996, 17.

Davis, Jack. "Yadabooka" in *The First Born and Other Poems*. Sydney: Angus and Robertson, 1970, 21.

——. "Aboriginal Australia". *Classic Poetry Series*. PoemHunter.Com—The World's Poetry Archive. <http://www.PoemHunter.com>

——. "The First Born". *The First Born and Other Poems*. Sydney: Angus and Robertson, 1970, 1.

——. "The Dreamers". *Plays From Black Australia*. Ed. Justine Saunders. Sydney: Currency Press, 1989, 4-71.

——. "Let Go". *Classic Poetry Series*. PoemHunter.Com—The World's Poetry Archive. <http://www.PoemHunter.com>

Davis, Jack and Bob Hodge (Eds). *Aboriginal Writing Today*. Canberra: Australian Institute of Aboriginal Studies, 1985.

Douglas, Josie and Marg Bowman. Quoted in 'Indigenous Discourse', *To Talk Straight* by Anita Heiss. Published by Aboriginal States Press, 35. <http://www.aiatsis.gov.au/aboriginal_studies_press/order>

Gilbert, Kevin. "Black Policies" in Jack Davis and Bob Hodge (Eds). *Aboriginal Writing Today*. Canberra: Australian Institute of Aboriginal Studies, 1985, 41.

——. *Living Black*. Melbourne: Penguin, 1978, 2.

——. "Better Blacks" in *People are Legends*. St. Lucia, 1978, 26-27.

——. *End of Dreamtime*. Sydney, 1971.

——. "Aboriginal Query" in *People are Legends*. St. Lucia, 1978, 48.

——. "Look, Koori" in *People are Legends*. St. Lucia, 1978, 52.

Hill, Roland Paul. "Blackfellas and Whitefellas: Aboriginal Land Rights, The Mabo Decision, and the Meaning of the Land." *Human Rights Quarterly*. 17.2, 1995, 303-22.

Howard, Shana. 'Solid Rock (Sacred Ground)' on the album 'Spirit of Place' by *Goanna*, W.E.A 600127, Sydney, 1982.

McGuinness, Bruce. "The Politics of Aboriginal Literature", in Davis and Hodge, eds. *Aboriginal Writing Today*, Canberra: Australian Institute of Aboriginal Studies, 1985. 46-47.

Narogin, Mudrooroo. *Writing from the Fringe: A Study of Modern Aboriginal Literature in Australia*. South Yaara, Vic: Hyland House, 1990. 1.

Paul, John Pope. "The address given by His Holiness at the Meeting with Aboriginal and Strait Islander people at Alice Springs on 20 November 1986." Canberra, 1986. 4.

Shoemaker, Adam. *Black Words, Write Page: Aboriginal Literature 1929-1988*. Canberra: The Australian National University E-Press, 1989, reprint 1992. 2004.

——. "An Interview with Jack Davis", *Westerly*, Vol. 27, No. 4, December 1982. 116.

Stanner, W.E.H. *After the Dreaming*. Sydney, 1969. 25.

Walker, Kath. "Then and Now" in *My People,* (Milton, 1981). 91.

——. "We Are Going" in *My People,* (Milton, 1981). 91.

——. "The Past" in *My People,* (Milton, 1981). 92.

——. "Time is Running Out". Ed. Kevin Gilbert. *Inside Black Australia: An Anthology of Aboriginal Poetry*. Penguin Books: Ringwood, Vic. 1988. 197.

Watego, Cliff. "Backgrounds to Aboriginal Literature." Ed. Emmanuel S. Nelson. *Connections*. Canberra: Aboriginal Studies Press, 1988. 11.

Watson, Maureen. "Walk Tall" in *Black Reflections*. Watter Park, 1982. 15.

Wilde, William, Joy Hooton and Barry Andrews. *The Oxford Companion to Australian Literature*. 2nd ed. Melbourne: Oxford University Press, 1994. 17.

11

Counter History and Race War Discourse of the Stolen Generations in Doris Pilkington's *Follow the Rabbit-Proof Fence*

V. Kundhavi

> The history of some is not the history of others.... It will be learned that one man's Victory is another man's defeat, what looks like right, law, or obligation from the point of view of power looks like the abuse of power, violence, and exaction when it is seen from the viewpoint of the new discourse.
>
> —*Michel Foucault*

Foucault in his series of lectures titled, *Society Must Be Defended* parallels modern historical consciousness with race war. He designates race to be a stable historical divide which is linked to nationality. The discourse of race war emerged in the 17th century and has replaced old historiography documented by sovereign power. Race war divides the society and forces the oppressed to resist against the laws which have been implemented in the name of rights. These historic struggles have been authenticated as a race war discourse. This enumerates defeats more than victories and its "prophetic tone echoes exiles and servitude and calls for a fulfillment of a forgotten promise" (N. pag). This discourse during the 19th century contributed to the emancipation of the people and later the racist discourse replaced the historic struggle with the biological struggle for existence. Foucault analyzes the counter historical function of race war discourse in the modern age. Through this discourse the untold history of a race could be retrieved. Counter history reactivated the past to create distinctive knowledge and brought to light the subversive power of the silenced historical experience. The glorious victories were demolished and justified as unfair defeats.

This counter history of race war has been recorded by a few Aboriginal societies which records the dominant culture and its dominant culture and its sovereignty to be unjust. The literary textuality has been used by both the dominant powers and the resistant voices. Contradicting each other the dominant controlling structures have been used to manipulate the subalterns and paradoxically the subalterns have used their writings as a space of protest and have challenged the ideologies of oppressive hegemonies. In Australian literature until the 1950's the presence of its indigenous people have been ignored. Since 1960's the protest literature represented by Aboriginal people have been created a strong impact. The counter history contextualized by these Aboriginals has assumed the form of social activism. Australian aboriginal writings include life writings—biographies, memoirs, letters and autobiographies. Philip Morrisey affirms,

> The psychological and physical brutality which attended the expansion of European interests in Australia into 20th century is being documented in increasing detail and thoroughness in contemporary histories...[they] not only depict the events which accompanied the subjugation of a nation but also...introduce history into Aboriginal life. (11)

The dominant race has executed a crucial exploitation to the indigenous people of Australia in the politics of Aboriginal child abduction. This traumatic oppression has resulted in an absolute dispossession and dislocation to the Aboriginal population along with a loss to their culture.

> In Australia today there may be one hundred thousand people of Aboriginal descent who do not know their families or communities. They are the people, or the descendants of people, who were removed from their families by a variety of white people for a variety of reasons. They do not know where they come from; some do not even know they are of

> Aboriginal descent.... As they grew up, they were expected to think white, to act white, and in the end to be white. (1997 [1989]: ix)

These children were historically referred to as the Stolen Generation. The term 'Stolen Generation' refers to the Australian Aboriginals and some of the Torres Strait Islanders who in their childhood age have been removed from their families by the dominant European powers—government agencies, church missions and Australian Federal state and forcibly sent to institutions or adopted in non-aboriginal families. Though these children were to get exposed to 'Anglo-values' and 'work habits', paradoxically they were placed only in dormitories and trained as farm labourers and domestic servants.

The **Bringing them Home Report** submits the disadvantages of the Stolen Generations as:

- They are more likely to come to the attention of the police as they grow into adolescence.
- They are more likely to suffer low self-esteem, depression and mental illness.
- They are more vulnerable to physical, emotional and sexual abuse.
- They had been almost always taught to reject their Aboriginality and Aboriginal culture.
- They are unable to retain links with their land.
- They cannot take a role in the cultural and spiritual life of their former communities.
- They are unlikely to be able to establish their right to native title. (qtd. in. Wikipedia.org)

Follow the Rabbit-Proof Fence is an Australian novel written by Nugi Garimara named Doris Pilkington and published in 1996. It is a personal memoir depicting the life struggle of indigenous Australian mixed race female children from their families during the twentieth century. As members of the Stolen Generation the three girls: Molly (14)—author's mother; Daisy (11)—Molly's sister and their cousin Gracie (8) were removed from their families to the Moore River Native Settlement in Western Australia. The escape of the three girls back home by trekking nearly 2,400 kilometres home by being guided by the rabbit-proof fence—a massive pest-exclusion fence which stretched across Western Australia from north to south is the plot of this memoir: *Follow the Rabbit-Proof Fence*. Pilkington chronicles her mother and her aunts' escape as children. After their return and begetting children from men of the dominant culture, the children born to these aboriginals are again abducted of whom the novelist Doris Pilkington belongs to. Originally named Nugi Garimara, she hails from the indigenous Australian Jigalong tribal community. As a four year old girl similar to her mother she too was forcibly taken to the internment camp meant for cross-breed aboriginal children. Later transferred to a Christian mission where she was educated, she was also hypnotized to believe the aboriginal culture to be of evil. After being trained as a nursing aide Pilkington turned to be a documentary film-maker, and a journalist. The sequel, *Under the Wintamarra Tree* (2002), describes Pilkington's experiences at Moore River and subsequently at the Roelands Mission Farm. Her final book *Home to Mother* (2006), an adapted version of her bestselling 1996 novel *Follow the Rabbit-Proof Fence* aimed at younger readers.

The novel *Follow the Rabbit-Proof Fence* narrates the journey of the three girls escape without any maps but with the only guidance of the State Barrier Fence to navigate home. This life writing novel is divided into nine chapters titled as follows: The First Military Post, The Swan River Colony, The Decline of Aboriginal Society, From the Deserts They Came, Jigalong. The Journey South, The Moore River Native Settlement 1931, The Escape and the ninth and the last chapter titled What Happened to them? What are they now?

From the description of The First Military Post on the shores of Western Australia established by the English and to the inhuman abduction of the Aboriginal women to satisfy their sexual desires, Pilkington renders a historical account of the first European settlers in June 1829. The usurping of one million square miles of territorial land and naming it as, 'Swan

River Colony' reflects the strategies which the dominant culture had adopted. The settlers were strictly advised to 'Keep up their Englishness' that is to preserve the English culture and traditions of their nation. Gradually the aboriginal social structure was completely ruined by the dominant culture. Pilkington sums up the total loss of their culture as, "The Nyungar people who once walked tall and proud, now hung their head in sorrow" (17). The conflict between the dominant and the native culture residents led to the exploitation of the other.

In chapter 4 titled, "From the Deserts They Came" the novelist traces the shooting of an aboriginal for having stolen a white settler's cow. The dehumanizing attitude of the oppressor gets explicit when the white man casually expresses, "Just a blackfella". More than genocide the natives were exploited from adhering to their culture which Pilkington narrates as, "They tell us we gotta cover everything up, the wudgebulla (white men) don't like to see neked (naked)". The historical details of Ruppi and his family who were the first settlers at Jigalong has been historically documented by Pilkington. In chapter five titled, "Jigalong 1907-1931" the novelist narrates the life of Maude an aboriginal who got conceived and gave birth to a child whose father Thomas Craig worked as an inspector in the rabbit-proof fence. This child was the first half-caste child of the aboriginals who was named as 'Molly' by Craig. Molly, the mother of Pilkington was the first half-caste child of the Jigalong people. Two of her aunts too delivered half-caste children—Gracie and Daisy. The novelist documents two institutions which were established for aboriginal children of white fathers. In June 1930, Constable Priggs, who is a "Protector of Aborigines' abducts Molly, Gracie, and Daisy to the Moore River Native Settlement Perth. Priggs asserts that, they will grow up with a better outlook on life than back at their camp.

Pilkington strictly adheres to the historical reality. Similar to the abduction of these children, a firsthand report of an abducted child gets documented in the Report which records as follows:

> I was at the post office with my Mum and Auntie [and cousin]. They put us in the police station and said they were taking us to Broome. They put the mums in there as well.

> But when we'd gone [about ten miles (16 km)] they stopped, and threw the mothers out of the car. We jumped on our mothers' backs, crying, trying not to be left behind. But the policemen pulled us off and threw us back in the car. They pushed the mothers away and drove off, while our mothers were chasing the car, running and crying after us. We were screaming in the back of that car. When we got to Broome they put me and my cousin in the Broome lock-up. We were only ten years old. We were in the lock-up for two days waiting for the boat to Perth. (N. pag)

After travelling for hundreds of kilometers the girls arrive at the Moore River Settlement. The girls are placed under the custody of Miss Evans who is a staff of the dorms. "When entering the dormitories for the first time, they notice—the door [is] locked with chains and padlocks...bars on the windows... just like a gaol" (63). Even the place to rest was uncomfortable. They found the place to sleep too difficult for, "...sleep on the hard mattress...feeling cold and lonely" (64). Usually there were no sheets or pillow covers except on special occasions. Whenever there was an inspection. "On the windows there were no colourful curtains, just wire screens and iron bars. It looked more like a concentration camp than a residential school for Aboriginal children" (72). The mere sight of the institution made Molly resolve to escape. She was the one who encouraged her other sisters also to pick up the challenges and undo European undertaking. Molly was cognizant of the awful outcome if caught. The punishment bordered on heartlessness: "...seven days punishment with just bread and water. Mr. Johnson shaved their heads bald and made them parade around the compound so that everyone could see them. They got the strap too" (17). Still this could not deter the young girls. Without any map and barefoot, they were guided only by a rabbit-proof fence, one of those constructed to keep rabbits from destroying the farmlands. The young girls had to adapt various tactics to escape the White gaze, "The girls were clever enough to avoid routes near larger towns and...knew they that would have been too exposed to the white population and their where about would have been immediately reported to the local police" (xiv). Familiar with landscape, they were able to gather food and feed themselves. Still crossing the desert, many times they collapsed with heat and hunger.

Molly assumes the role of the leader and the three girls decide to walk to Jigalong by foot. They walk steadily through the wilderness. Their main goal was to find the rabbit-proof fence. During nights they stay in wilderness and at times even in rabbit burrows. The girls continue to beg for food and after nine weeks of continuous walking on bare foot they arrive at Jigalong and get reunited. Molly marries Toby Kelly and begets two daughters and again is taken to the Moore settlement, wherein after nine years Molly takes the same route to Jigalong. The historical oppression continues as her the children are stolen to the settlement reserves. Daisy leads her life as a domestic maid and Gracie is left behind in the settlement.

The journey of the three aboriginal girls depicts the history of resistance as facts of triumph and survival and empowerment. This memoir serves as an authentic document of social activism and the vivid description of the hazardous path establishes Aboriginal writing as a socially conscientious practice. "The... frightened and miserable girls began to cry, by the lamentation of their loved ones and the visions of them sitting on the ground in their camp letting their tears mix with the red blood that flowed from the cuts on their heads" (*Rabbit-Proof Fence*, 45). The child abduction proves to be an irreparable loss of relationships. The whole process has lead the aboriginals to experience pain and anguish. The brutal inhuman act of the dominant powers gets inhibited under Church mission control or sent to government institutions. Pilkington states this merciless plight as, "Every mother of part Aboriginal child was aware that their offspring could be taken away from them at any time and they were powerless to stop the abductors. That is why many women preferred to give birth in the bush rather than in a hospital where they believed their babies would be taken from them soon after birth" (40-41).

Numerous Aboriginal issues have been brought by the Australian women writers of Aboriginal descent. Their works stand as testimonies which depict the atrocities executed by the whites on their native people. Amanda Nettle beck in her essay, "Presenting Aboriginal Women's Life Narratives" asserts that these writings serve as, "not only testimonies of individual experience but also records accounts of mission life, government surveillance, stolen childhoods, and other forms of twentieth century race politics" (43). Pilkington writes, "The task of reconstructing the trek home from the settlement has been both an exhausting and interesting experience. One needed to have a vivid imagination" (xi). Writings by Aboriginal writers serve the purpose of insurrection of subjugated knowledge to which writers like Doris Pilkington, Sally Morgan and Kim Scott belong to. Doris Pilkington claims the honour of writing 'her story' through the authentication of historicism.

Works Cited

Nettelbeck, Amanda. "Presenting Aboriginal Women's Life Narratives". *New Literatures Review*, 34 (1997): 43-56.

Macey, David. Society library Must Be defended. http://rebels-.org/files/foucault_society_must_be_defended.pdf

Morrissey, Philip. "Restoring a Future to a Past." Ed. Anna Rutherford. *Aboriginal Culture Today.* Sydney: Dangaroo Press, 1998. 10-15.

Pilkington, Doris. *Follow the Rabbit-Proof Fence.* St Lucia: University of Queensland Press, 1996.

http://www.nsdc.org.au/stolen-generations/history-of-the-stolen-generations/the-history-of-the-stolen-generations.

http://en.wikipedia.org/wiki/Stolen_Generations.

12

Rebellion against the Culture of Stoicism and the Land in A.D. Hope's "Australia"

Ravindra Kumar

The basic Australian literary tradition is a compound of sound learning, rebelliousness, ardent faith in the common man, and an even more ardent faith in the Australian future (C. Hartley Grattan in *Introducing Australia*, New York, 1942).

The origin of Australian Poetry lays in the prison system. It was an outcome of the emotional turmoil the convicts were suffering in the prisons. By expressing their empathy through an artistic medium, the convicts were trying to maintain a degree of emotional distance from their turmoil as well as that of their friends. From this very foundation, a rich poetic tradition took birth on the Australian land. Basic Australian poetry is the poetry of anguish and rebellion but it also glorifies the nation. Poets like Kenneth Slessor who wrote during the war period portrayed a conflict between stoicism and anguish through their poems. Another poet Les Murray is also very critical of the Australian society as he revolts against the stoic culture of Australia.

A.D. Hope is another name in this line of Australian Poetry who is considered as one of the most influential and celebrated Australian poets of the twentieth century. He began his career as a lecturer at the University of Melbourne in 1945, and in 1951 he got the fortune to become the first Professor of English at the newly-founded Canberra University College. In 1968, he was appointed Emeritus Professor at the Australian National University. He also served as an Officer of the Order of the British Empire in 1972 and a Companion of the Order of Australia in 1981. Although he started writing at the age of 23 but his first collection of poems "The Wandering Islands" came out in 1955. Satire, lyricism, philosophical meditation and cheerful eroticism are the major concerns in his poetry. Some of his poems are metaphysical, sensual, serious, frivolous, mocking and mystical in nature. A number of critics recognize him as a classic poet who incorporates mythology, legends, and fables in his poetry. Despite the anachronistic nature of his poetry, critics praise his bitter satire and clarity of language which makes him an important figure in contemporary poetry. His poetic theory has forced many critics to view his verse as neoclassical, obsolete and too conservative. But in recent years, critics have reevaluated his verse, and have found great value in his formalized style. Critics have also noted a dearth of any identifiable Australian material in most of his work and perceive him as an outsider within the tradition of Australian literature. Eroticism and sexuality are the major concerns in the poetry of Hope; the theme of male chauvinism also runs deeply in many of his poems. But, despite being called old-fashioned and sexist by critics, his poetry continues to be anthologized and studied all over the world. It shows that as a poet, Hope's literary reputation remains strong. As an author Hope is a storyteller, teacher and an enchanter, the three attributes that Vladimir Nabokov considered essential in a writer. Kevin Hart states that "when A.D. Hope died in 2000 at the age of 93, Australia lost its living poet (Kevin Hart, A.D. Hope in the *Oxford Australian Writers Series*).

Hope is very critical of Australia and its society, culture, tradition and its people. Sometimes he is full of appreciation for Australia, but mainly he seems to be critical of the land. The aim of present paper is to show rebellion against the culture of stoicism and the land in the poem Australia by A.D. Hope. Hope shows a large amount of scope on his ability to comment on Australian society, its landscape and the forces shaping it. Although many of his poems glorify the country, some contain the themes of rebellion, not against authorities but against the culture of stoicism and the land itself. The poem shows bitter criticism of Australia and its people. Hope had been a frequent visitor and explorer of the eastern Australian land in his later years. This poem is most probably a result of his observations of this particular Australian area. The poem contains seven stanzas, each stanza consisting of four lines with the rhyme scheme (Ab ab). The first stanza portrays Australia as "a nation of trees, drab green and desolate grey" that "darkens her hills". Here Australia is presented as a bleak and almost colorless nation because everything in it is dull and without any color. This deterioration resembles the "field uniform of modern wars" where almost all the objects are in shade of "endless, outstretched paws of Sphinx demolished or stone lion worn away".

The field is equivalent to the modern wars and the mountains are thick and dark. The Sphinx is a mythical figure with human's head and the body of a lion laying outside Thebes, asking travellers a riddle and killing them if is not answered. It killed itself when King Oedipus solved the riddle. The Sphinx is seen as a creature of great wisdom. This comparison is directly linked to Hope's vision of Australia which was at her intellectual height once upon a time. But now the glorious past has faded away and the reputation of Australia has considerably declined. The next stanza presents a negative image of Australia. The poet feels that the people who consider Australia a young nation are not giving the real picture of the land. Rather they, according to Hope, lie. It is an old country and "the last of lands, the emptiest". It is "a woman beyond her change of life, a breast still tender but within the womb is dry". The lines suggest that Australia may be considered a young nation by the world's standards, yet it is the most empty. It can be compared to a woman who is fresh and alert outwardly but from the inside is empty as it possesses nothing.

She has tender feelings but her womb is dry. The poet feels that Australia is devoid of internal beauty. In the next stanza, Hope calls Australia a land that is devoid of culture. To him Australia is "without songs, architecture and history" where the "rivers of water drown among inland sands, the river of her immense stupidity". Hope feels that Australia has neither any culture to boast of nor any historical background nor culture to speak off. Yet he feels that it has the capabilities to do so. However, the ideas are drowned among "inland sands". The poet portrays a true picture of Australia that is a barren and empty land. It is able to sustain life but almost unable to produce it. This is evident from the fact as he blames the detractors for the slow erosion of Australia, where it has turned into a country that is no longer as wise as it used to be once upon a time. The island sand dries all the water which he calls "the river of her immense stupidity". This reflects Hope's patriotic feelings for his nation where, the poet feels, Australia is a victim of circumstances. The very next portrayal of Australia is very bleak as it is portrayed as a nation that is nothing at all and where there are "monotonous tribes from Cairns to Perth". The poet feels that before the colonization of Australia, monotonous tribes lived here. Large number of people arrived from Cairns to Perth city. He is more critical about the Australian people showing them monotonous tribes who boast not of living but rather boast of merely surviving.

In the next stanza, the poet compares the five main cities of Australia to "five teeming sores." Perhaps the poet is trying to affirm that the people who move here are rather unwelcome, and they are "second hand Europeans" that give birth rapidly on these "alien shores." He sees these inhabitants as people for "drain" Australia, a "vast parasite robber state." This could be well connected to Australia's past history when it was Great Britain's exile island. Dangerous and hard core criminals were sent here in exile instead of sending them to the prisons. Hope is most probably trying to put forth that the newcomers coming to Australia are like giant leeches that take in all that is good in the country. It simply means that Australia is reduced to a vast parasite robber-state that breeds a timid race of second hand Europeans.

Unfortunately these mediocre citizens have become the heroes of the nation now. His notions of patriotism are well reflected in the last two stanzas where he feels that there are "some like me (him) who turn gladly home" to withdraw from the "lush jungle of modern thought" in order to seek the "Arabian desert of the human mind." The poet enjoys retreating from the materialistic mundane world and wishes to stay in a rather desert. It means that all the above-mentioned detractions can be considered as additional benefits of being an Australian. Here Hope seems to paradoxically redeem Australia and hopes for a savage and scarlet sprit which will spring from the bush country tradition. The last two lines need special attention of readers where Hope states "the learned doubt, the chatter of cultured apes" which is merely called civilization without it really being so. The poet presents a vivid image of Australia and states that in the name of growth and civilization, they have buried their own culture. The intellectual development of Australia is being done at the cost of their own true culture. Perhaps he explores with a negative and myopic approach and presents the spiritual barrenness of the land.

Reading the poem from the 20th century context gives us an entirely different meaning. The poem makes less sense now that the second hand Europeans is now just a proportion of the melting pot of cultures: multi-cultural society. What the poet misses in the poem is the distinct style of art, architectural society and culture for which Australia is well known all over the world.

The poem has seven stanzas, each stanza consisting of four lines with the rhyme scheme AbAb. The first five stanzas state how Australia is both a new and old country-geologically old politically new. The stanzas also state how it is both European colonial and naturally individual.

Hope was of the view that poetry was philosophical music, and his works dramatize the ways in which a philosophical argument is best represented by analogy. He believed that all great poems include within their music an argument of some kind. Australia is one such poem in which he assumes that the land may be rich and prosperous on the surface but beneath it lays distortion of culture and tradition. Though the poem received much criticism but it remains one of his most discussed poems even today.

Works Cited

Hart, Kevin. "A.D. Hope" in the *Oxford Australian Writers Series*. Melbourne: Oxford University Press, 1992.

Hooton, Joy W. *A.D. Hope*. Melbourne: Oxford University Press, 1979.

Hope, A.D. "Poems". London: Hamish Hamilton, 1960.

Kermode, Frank. "Poetry in Australia". *Manchester Guardian*, March 1961.

13

Judith Wright: Perspective from Nation, Love and Death

Kartika Prakash Dubey

The romantic idea that true humanity must be meditated by a deep involvement in one's unique culture led to an admiration for songs, poems, stories, plays and other creation understood as emanation of the national soul. The language of the people was accorded a unique value, no less as the medium of cultural self-expression than as a practical rule of thumb about how far the boundaries of a putative nation might stretch (Minogue 551).

Above context is very appropriate for Judith Wright who begins her poetic journey through her first anthology entitled *The Moving Image* (1946) as someone deeply in love with the Australia, her people, her landscape and the intermingling between the two. For her, poetry is, "a human creative activity" and "not an academic subject of study" (Wright vii). Her genuine concern for man, now a machine, over—fervent about, "the new days reel/of punched instruction" (Wright 15).

Her early poetry is primarily concerned with "an intense evocation of the spirit of the place". She, a distinguished Australian practitioner of poetic art, focused to our vision—the problems of human relationships, pollution—physical emotional, dehumanization which results in decline of our inner and other worlds.

Similarly, Faulkner made his fictions at Yoknapatawpha country the microcosmic representation of the American South.

Tarashankar Bandopadhyay, the Bengali novelist, also made his representation of "Rar Bangla" as the Symbol of Indian Society so did Judith Wright. Sights, sounds and scenarios of her New England home becomes a representative embodiment of Australia, her own "Blood's Country".

Veronica Brandy biographer of Judith Wright aptly states that Judith becomes gradually conscious of "a sense of sacredness in the land" wrights is of the opinion that one should pay attention to "what they say and imply, rather than the way they convey it." But in her poetry we cannot ignore the "Way" of saying because "arts are the supreme form of communicative activity" (Richards, 97):

> "South of My Day's Circle" gives us the vision as:
>
> South of my day's circle
>
> I know it dark against the stars, The high lean country.
>
> Full of old stories that still go walking in my sleep. (First Anthology *The Moving Image*)

These lines are celebrating an Australia which is covered with the Misty aura of oral narratives, native myths and stories that have the capacity of constantly haunting an ardent lover of this rugged, aged country where life is harsh but the fruits of labour are sweet enough.

She writes in her autobiography a *Half of Lifetime* (1999) while she was returning home to her pastoral form "at the admonitions of her father for her active help to run the affairs of farm". As the train panted up the foothills of the land the haze of dust and eucalypt vapor dimmed the drought-stricken landscape, I found myself suddenly and sharply aware of it as "my country" these hills and valleys well—not mine, but me; the treat of Japanese invasion hung over them as over me; I felt it under my ribs. Whatever other blood I held, that was the country I loved and knew (wsws.org).

Though her return to farm house resulted in discontinuation of her studies but provided her a rare chance of interacting with the farm worker and loving them. They opened the rare gateway of Australia's untold history and unrecorded plights of the common people, its myths and folklores, its rich cultural heritage for Judith Wright. Their life story gave her the realization of the true story of tyranny and mass carnage inflicted upon the Aborigines, the true owners of the land, by the British Settlers. She also realized that her own forefathers were as much responsible for the dispossession of the Aborigines.

In this research paper, I wish to focus upon the decision of Judith Wright to use poetry as a rapier to defend the right of these marginalized subalterns, to hasten in the Australian psyche a feeling of solidarity, where everyone contributes to the development of the nation and most importantly to save the honor of the land. She creates in her poetry, as David Malouf aptly claims, the tension of an oppositional pull between "environment and place on one hand, and on the other, all the complex associations of an inherited culture" (wsws.org).

Historical perspective justifies that nationalism developed as opposed to cosmopolitanism which aims at Universalistic rationalism.

Omar Frantz Fanon (1925-61) a stalwart and acclaimed Algerian revolutionary who has cited an essay entitled "The Pitfalls of National Consciousness" focuses upon resistance against colonialism. He is less of preacher and practitioner. He like, Leela Gandhi, actually hastened a new momentum to the nationalistic struggle in colonies as:

> Although Fanon's writings maintain a deep ambivalence towards the political desirability of the entrenched and centralized postcolonial nation-state, he remains unequivocally committed to the therapeutic necessity of anti-colonial national agitation.... Fanon privileges nationalism for its capacity to heal the historical wounds inflicted by the 'Manichean' structure of colonial culture which confines the colonized o a limited, barely human existence. In this context, of regaining an Edenic wholeness. It becomes a process of territorialisation and repossession which replace the 'two-fold citizenship' of colonial culture and with a radically unified counter-culture. (Gandhi, 111-12)

They were those who close to adapt themselves to the new environment rather than superimpose their class value of

Englishness upon it. They were.... Set against the squattocarcy. And underwent a convulsive change in social values and patterns and from them come not only an authentic patriotic fervor, but a tradition of warmth, hospitality and egalitarianism (wsws.org).

As the train panted up the foothills of the Moonbis and the haze of dust and eucalypt vapour dimmed the drought-stricken landscape, I found myself suddenly and sharply aware of it as 'my country'. These hill and valleys were—not mine, but me; the treat of Japanese invasion hung over them as over me; I felt it under my ribs. Whatever other blood I held, that was the country I loved and knew (wsws.org).

Thus, we find her poetry breathes about the recreation of the Australian landscape. Her Bullocky, The Kite, The Ancient Cycade one the poems of love as divine feeling. J.W. attempts Universal themes like love life death nature nation religion was, etc.

Heredity poetry is primarily concerned with an intuitive evocation of spirit of place.

South of my day's circle,
I know it dark against the stars, the high lean country
Full of old stories that still go walking in my sleep.

The Inescapable association between nature and man comes full circle through this symbolic realization.

Her Second Anthology *Woman to Man* tells about the material Maternal Love and identification with the child's growth in womb of there but in deeper dimension poem speaks about the relationship of nation and her inhabitants.

I wither and you break from me;
Yet though you dance in living night
I am the earth, I am the roof,
I am the stem that fed the fruit,
The link that joins you to the night.
Glassed with cold deep sleep and dazzled by the moon,
Out of the confused hammering dark of the train
I looked and saw under the moon's cold sheet

Your dedicate dry breasts, country that build my heart;
And the small trees on their uncolored slope
Like poetry moved, articulate and sharp
Draw from the flying dark its breath of dew
Till the unloving come to life in you.

In her own way she has taken a step further for us in the expression of Australian national, spiritual and environmental values in her poetry (wsws.org).

She wrote purely passionate intensely personal and feminine love poems follow as:

None but I shall know you
as none but I have known;
yet there is death and a maiden
who wait for you alone;.....
so move in me my darling,
whose debt I cannot pay,
pain and the dark must claim you,
and passion and the day. ("Woman's Song")

Following lines reflect the mystery of recreation and reproduction, felt me as process of life and directed to one end:

Her Second Book *Woman to Man* differs from other poets in the treatment of the theme of love.

This is no child with a child's face,
this has no name to name it by;
yet you and I have known it well.
This is our hunter and our chase,
the third who lay in our embrace,...
This is the strength that your arm knows,
The arc of flesh that is my breast,
The precise crystals of our eyes,
This is the blood's wild tree that grows
The intricate and folded rose. (*Woman to Man*)

Thus, we find that quiet passion is the dominant feature of her poems. They share unspectacular infrastructure, unity and creation are the hallmarks of her feminine and motherly feeling. Her *Woman to Child* incarnates the dream of the birth of a child and sets a conversation:

> You who were darkness warmed my flesh
> where out of darkness rose the seed.
> Then all a world I made in me;
> all the world you hear and see
> hung upon my dreaming blood.

Remarkable identification with Mother Earth:

> I wither and you break from me;
> Yet though you dance in living light
> I am the earth, I am the roof,
> I am the stem that fed the fruit,
> The link that joins you to the night,
> exhales towards Universal Madonna.

Death is also one of the fundamental themes in *Midnight* of Judith Wright. It is all about death and rebirth as eternal twins in mode of Christian theology of resurrection which follows death:

> Because I could not stop for death,
> He kindly stopped for me;
> The carriage held but just ourselves
> And immortality....
> Since then 'tis centuries; but each
> Feels shorter than the day
> I first surmised the horses' heads
> Were towards eternity.

A close resemblance:

> As a plant in winter dies
> down into the germ, and lies
> Leafless, tongue less, lost in earth
> imaging its fierce rebirth;..........
> and with the whirling rays of the Sun
> and shuttle stroke of living rain
> weaves that image from its heart
> and like a god is born again.

It holds universal significance, a kind of cyclic process which is inherent in life and sings the lore of, "If Winter Comes Can spring be far behind"?

Syndrome of Eros—Thanatos delineated through the concept of Love and Death:

My eyes-rest upon you,
To me eyes turn,
As bee goes to honey,
As fire to fire will burn........
But so silent my heart falls
When you are away
I can hear the world breathing
Where he hides from our day. ("Our Love is So Natural")

Spiritual union is exemplified through two acres:

Where in predestined joy
And with a shock like death,
The two halves of my being
Met to make one truth...
Yet where the circle was joined
The desperate chase began,
Where love in love dissolved
Sprang up the woman-man

Her implication is obvious: a poet has an artistic-cum-social duty to perform. Last but not the least:

The country grows
Into the image of the people
And the people grow
Into the likeness of the country
Till to the soul's geographer
Each becomes the symbol of the other. (Max Dann)
The blacksmith's boy hung the rainbow on his shoulder
Instead of his broken gun.
Lizards ran out to see,
Snakes made way for him,
And the rainbow shone as brightly as the sun.
(Wollman, 75)

Works Cited

Gandhi, Leela. *Postcolonial Theory: A Critical Introduction.* New Delhi: Oxford India Paperback, 2004.

Minogue. "Kenneth Nationalism". Kuper, Adam and Kuper, Jessica (eds). *The Social Science Encyclopaedia*. London: Routledge, 1989.

Richards, I.A. *The Principles of Literary Criticism*. New York: Routledge and Kegan Paul, 1929. 17.

Said, Edward. *Culture and Imperialism*. New York: Vintage Books, 1993.

Wright, Judith. *Fourth Quarter*. London: Angles and Robertson, 1976.

——. *Because I was Invited*. Melbourne: Oxford University Press, 1975. vii.

Wsws: Arts Review: *Literature and Poetry*.

14

Writing the Self: Australian Women Autobiographies

(With Special Reference to Sally Morgan's *My Place* and Glenyse Ward's *Wandering Girl*)

Arzoo Naqvi

At the time of colonization in 1788, Australian Aborigines had not developed a system of writing, their reflection in the literature before settlement was unfavourable. Early accounts by the English buccaneer William Dampier wrote of the "Natives of New Holland" as being "barbarous savages"; but Captain James Cook accounts of Aborigines were sympathetic:

> these people may truly be said to be in the pure state of nature, and may appear to some to be the most wretched upon the earth; but in reality they are far happier than...we Europeans. (Wildey, 2)

Non-Indigenous representations of Aboriginal people are to be found in the history of Australian literature; Aboriginal texts as literature, history and historiography; postcolonial theory and interpretation; Aboriginal cinema and its relation to the emergence of Aboriginal writing and cultures; oral histories and questions of transcription and translation; publishing contexts, audiences and autonomy; questions of cross-cultural understanding and reconciliation.

With the arrival of the nineteenth century and the development of an Australian literature written by European settlers, the Aborigine became a common feature for them. David Collins in *An Account of the English Colony in New South Wales* (1798), described that by the end of April 1788 violence between Aborigines and settlers had broken out.

Black writing in Australia has been suppressed and dominated by the white, after a long journey of struggle Aboriginal writing in Australia emerged in 1924 with the work of David Unaipan, who was the first published black Australian author. His emergence was the beginning of a black literary tradition in Australia. Black writing became a tool for Aboriginals with which they fight their battle for justice and recognition. Suppression gave the tongue to Aboriginal women authors and they wrote their experiences for being Aboriginal and for women.

Autobiography is a biography of the self, the question that rises while analyzing an autobiography concern the way the writer perceives herself in her autobiography. Autobiography comes to the question of life story of Australian Aboriginal women; the question became more prominent, because their stories or autobiographies revolve around the issue of identity. The voice of Aboriginal women was unheard, but now telling of past experiences, alienation and adversity have helped them to overcome it. The Aboriginal female autobiographies such as those of Ward and Sally Morgan reflect the culture of dispossession, sexual molestation, story of the stolen children and untold sufferings and pain.

Morgan's *My Place* tells the history of Aboriginal people which needs to be told to rebuild Aboriginal culture and identity. Jody Broun said, "Morgan's book is an eye opener to a shameful past many white Australians would sooner ignore or forget. In delivering a blackened history which presents the injustice committed against Aboriginal people" (Broun, 26).

My Place comes as a postcolonial autobiography foregrounded with racial, Aboriginal class and gender concerns, exploring the nexus between Aboriginal resistance and the white institutions of subjugation and oppression. The chief protagonists of this novel Gladys and Daisy are representative of the stolen generations, Aboriginality or marginality racism, who interprets the harsh exploitation and repercussion of the oppressor's manifestation of power on the identity of the individual. Morgan emphasizes in her novel, that Aboriginal females were subsumed by the superior male colonizers, Gladys and Nan both being subject to this and tried to hide their Aboriginal identity and forced to deny Sally to tell her roots

"Tell them you are an Indian" (Morgan, 38)

The success of *My Place* became a trendsetter and was followed by many Aboriginal writer and Aboriginal women's autobiographies.

Sally's *My Place* also exposed miscegenation and sexual exploitation of Aboriginal women by the implication of Drake-Brockman as Nan's father and perhaps Glady's father as well:

> Arthur threw back his head and laughed, then he thumped his fist on the arm of his chair and said, 'Now you listen to me, Daisy's father is the same as mine. Daisy is my only full sister. Albert, he's our half brother, his father was Howden, too, but by a different woman.... Too right! Now, about this Maltese Sam, don't forget Alice was Howden's second wife and they had the Victorian way of thinking in those days... but later after he married his first wife, Nell, he changed our names. He did not want to own us no more.... No white man wants to have black kids running round the place with his name.' (157)

In simple prose Glenyse Ward too gives account of her life after removal in her autobiography *Wandering Girl*. It is a text about a stolen aboriginal girl who was taken away from her mother because she was a half cast. The story is focused on the period of her life when she was working for the Bigelow family. When she was baby, she was taken from her Nyoongarvii parents to St. John of God's orphanage in Rivervale, Perth. At the age of three she was moved to Wandering, short for St Francis Xavier Native Mission at Wandering Brook was treated like a slave. She had to grow up with humiliation from the whole family, especially from Mrs. Bigelow who talked to her scornfully all the time.

A note at the end of the 1995 edition reveals that "when her mother took her to the Doctor's when she was one year old; she was taken away by Native Welfare as her mother was Deemed unfit." The opening page text illustrates the pain of stolen generation:

> You see in the early days of survival and struggle, there was a lot of hardship and agony amongst the Aboriginal people. Through the misguided minds of earnest white people we were taken away from our natural parents. This affected all of us. *We lost our identity* through being put into missions, forced to abide by the European way. (Ward, 1)

Ward discusses the issues of Aboriginal Identity. She discusses and comments on the Aboriginal situation and identifies herself as an Aboriginal girl. According to her she is a black domestic. She gets inspiration from a white worker to protest against her white mistress. Her racist bosses call her their "dark slave" to sniggers from people in town. Ward asserts that Wandering Girl is her story, she tells of her life from the age of sixteen, when she left Wandering Mission, her 'home' since the age of three, to work for a white family in the rural districts of the south-west of Western Australia during the 1960s. Ward utilizes the opportunity of telling her story to create an image of herself as someone who has survived an unpleasant past without any bitterness or hostility towards 'white' Australians. In interviews, in Aboriginal Voices, Wards states:

> If we bring up our kids the right way and set them in the right frame of mind and let them know that we're all the same—that there's no-one different in this world, that we're all the same whether black or white—then if we can get that through their heads and everyone else's that we should all live as one race...well, that would be a good thing now, wouldn't it? (Ward)

However Ward manages to keep a positive attitude about her future. She also tells us of the people who made her life better with their gestures of kindness: Bill the older worker on the farm; the lady who owned the sweet shop in town; and her fellow orphans who are also placed on farms as servants.

Aboriginal women writers offer resistance in their autobiographies to the domination they suffer as women, as Aboriginal women and as Aboriginies. In her *Sister Girl*, Jackie Huggins discusses the multiple voices of Aboriginal women writers in their autobiographies:

> As women we have all been subject to divide and rule socialization, and racist and sexist ideologies. However, the overwhelming evidence and the experience of Aboriginal women points to the fact that Aboriginal women remain discriminated against due to their race rather than their gender. For example, a cosmetically apparent Aboriginal woman is regularly stereotyped on the basis of being a boong, coon, nigger, gin or abo far in excess of being a "woman". The lack of recognition and real understanding of this political difference is a major issue still to be resolved by the white women's movement. (Huggins, 25)

The genre of life writing has become an extremely important source for human rights campaigns since many of the personal, eye witnessed accounts tell of human rights violations. Aboriginal women write about the efforts they are prepared to take in order to document the past for their family and for whole community. They want to make their life experience a public knowledge in order to acquaint others with the suppressed histories of native people during colonization.

Works Cited

Broun, Jody. Whose Place? *A Study of Sally Morgan's My Place*. Pymble, NSW, Australia: Angus and Robertson, 1992.

Huggins, Jackie. *Sister Girl*. St Lucia, Qld.: University of Queensland Press, 1998.

Morgan, Sally. *My Place*. Western Australia: Fremantle Art Center Press, 1987.

Ward. Interview 'Glenyse Ward: Writer', 23.

Ward, Glenyse. *Wandering Girl*. Broome: Magabala Books, 1987.

15

Ada Cambridge's *An Answer*: A Re-Study of Post-Colonialism and an Australian Poem

Jaba Kusum Singh

Poetry, it is said, predate literacy. It is known to all that epic poetry, from the Indian *Vedas* that dates back as early as 1700-1200 BC and Zoroaster's *Gathas* to the *Odyssey* in 800 to 675 BC, appears to have been composed in poetic form to give support to memorization and oral spread, in prehistoric and ancient societies. It cannot be also denied that other forms of poetry developed directly from folk songs.

The students of literature know it well that the oldest surviving epic poem is the *Epic of Gilgamesh*, from the 3rd millennium BC in Sumer that is Mesopotamia and now Iraq, which was written in cuneiform script on clay tablets and, later, papyrus. Apart from this, the other ancient epic poetry includes the Greek epics *Iliad* and *Odyssey*, the Old Iranian books the *Gatha, Avesta* and *Yasna*, the Romannational epic, Virgil's *Aeneid*, and of course the *Ramayana* and *Mahabharata*.

When one studies the aesthetics of poetry that is poetics, one cannot neglect that the Classical Chinese poetry in the case of the *Shijing* (*Classic of Poetry*), records the development of poetic norms with ritual and aesthetic importance. While studying poetry scholars down the ages have struggled to find a definition that could encompass formal differences as great as those between Chaucer's *Canterbury Tales* and Matsuo Bashō's

Oku no Hosomichi, as well as differences in context spanning Tanakhreligious poetry, love poetry, and rap.

When one peeps into the studies of the classical thinkers one finds that they have employed classification as a way to define and assess the quality of poetry. Particularly, the existing fragments of Aristotle's *Poetics* describe three genres of poetry—the epic, the comic, and the tragic—and develop rules to distinguish the highest-quality poetry in each genre, based on the underlying purposes of the genre. Later aestheticians and critics acknowledged three major genres: epic poetry, lyric poetry, and dramatic poetry, for they treated comedy and tragedy as subgenres of dramatic poetry.

Aristotle's work was influential throughout the Middle East during the Islamic Golden Age, as well as in Europe during the Renaissance. Later poets and aestheticians often distinguished poetry from prose, as the critics maintained that prose writing is a type of script that has an appetite to logical explication and a linear narrative structure which is not dissimilar in every way from poetry.

This does not entail that poetry is unreasonable or be deficient in narration, but rather that poetry is an attempt to render the beautiful or sublime without the burden of appealing the logical or narrative deliberation process. English Romantic poet John Keats termed this escape from logic "Negative Capability". This "romantic" loom outlook form as a central element of successful poetry because form is abstract and discrete from the underlying imaginary logic. This approach remained influential up till the 20th century.

But as all know twentieth century is a happening period and thus during this period, there was also substantially more interaction among the various poetic traditions, in part because of the spread of European colonialism and the abundant rise in global trade. In addition to this the boom in translation brought into focus numerous ancient works.

Twentieth century is also a time when several literary and philosophical theories made its presence felt. A major controversy emerged between those thinkers for whom the poet is a creator and those who were not ready to accept that poetry is just a simple creative act like other media. Yet other modernists challenge the very attempt to define poetry as misguided.

The rejection of traditional forms and structures for poetry that began in the first half of the 20th century corresponded with the puzzling of the purpose and meaning of traditional definitions of poetry and of differences between poetry and prose, predominantly given examples of poetic prose and prosaic poetry. Many modernist poets have written in non-traditional forms or in what traditionally would have been considered prose, although their writing was generally infused with poetic expression and often with rhythm and tone established by non-metrical means. On one hand, there was a considerable formalist reaction within the modernist schools on the other hand, there was a breakdown of structure, and that gave impetus to the development of new formal structures and synthesis as on the revival of older forms and structures.

The postmodernism, now has come to convey more completely prose and poetry as distinct entities, and also among genres of poetry, as having meaning only as cultural artifacts. Postmodernism goes beyond modernism's stress on the creative role of the poet, to emphasize the role of the reader of a text, and to highlight the complex cultural web within which a poem is read. Today, throughout the world, poetry often integrates poetic form and diction from other cultures and from the past, further baffling attempts at definition and classification that were once sensible within a tradition such as the Western canon.

Postmodernism and postcolonialism compliments each other. Poetry now is a culmination of many things and it is truer when one reads and tries to understand poetries of the colonial countries that focus on colonial tradition and heart squeezing subjugations. The scholars of literature knows it well that post colonialism or postcolonial studies is an academic discipline that have characteristic methods of intellectual discourse which analyze, explain, and respond to the cultural bequests of colonialism and imperialism, to the human consequences of controlling a country and establishing settlers for the economic exploitation of the native people and their land.

As already mentioned, illustrating from postmodern schools of thought, postcolonial studies study the politics of knowledge that includes creation, control, and distribution by considering the useful relations of social and political power that uphold colonialism and neocolonialism. This means it examines the how and the why of an imperial regime's representations, including social, political and cultural, of the imperial colonizer and of the colonized people.

As the most prominent genre of contemporary history, postcolonialism questions and reinvents the modes of cultural perception. It questions the ways of viewing and of being viewed. Critics say that like anthropology, postcolonialism records human relations among the colonial nations and the subaltern peoples exploited by colonial rule. Postcolonialism presents, explains, and illustrates the ideology and the praxis of neocolonialism, with examples drawn from the humanities. It presents the stories of colonial subjugation of the subaltern man and woman. When one concentrates on Australian literature one cannot deny the effect of colonial rule on its literary quest and thus the upshot is obviously a literature that is highly impressed by postmodernism as well as post colonialism.

Australia was a British colony from 1788 to 1901, and during this period settlers from Europe slowly began to define themselves as a people with a distinct national identity, reflected in the literature they produced. Initially, Australian writers relied on literary models borrowed from European, and especially British sources. This cultural belief was also reflected in the economic life of Australia, as those who held arable land, called squatters, imitated the landed aristocracy in England. The result was the creation of a social divide between the privileged landowners and the lower classes—migrants, laborers, and especially convicts, the first Australian colonists, who had been transported to British penal settlements on the continent's eastern coast. As the years passed, convict and settler narratives appeared, as did scattered lyrics and ballads composed by amateur poets. Nonetheless, critics lamented the perceived lack of any first-rate literature by Australians during the first half of the nineteenth century.

The early Australian poets whose works are prominently read are Charles Harper, Adam Lindsay Gordon, Henry Kendall. The predominating subject of their poem were the solitude and grandeur of a landscape that dwarfs its people, there are poets who also concentrated on lyricism but poet like Gordon wrote poems of action and thus is famous as the poet of ordinary men.

The richness, potency and vivacity of Australian poetry are noticeable by its exceptional diversity. Yet themes continue through this diversity. An abiding interest is the Australian landscape and how to relate to it—its presence and its visual power. Appreciably, a great deal of modern Australian poetry has been innovative and experimental, whether consciously or not. The search for innovation itself had stressed in its explorations.

Ada Cambridge is one such poet who was born in the English fen country, at St. Germans, in Norfolk, in 1844. Belonging to a strictly religious family she primarily wrote hymns based on moral and religious subjects. Her early works are the result of her lifelong insistence on and pursuit of physical, spiritual and moral reliability. The uniqueness of her literary works is the amalgamation of poetry and prose.

The poem *An Answer* is a short but highly thoughtful piece of art first published in her short collection of poems entitled *Unspoken Thoughts* in 1887. The collection was first published unnamed because it was a bundle of fiery, revolutionary feministic thoughts. It is shock not only to her clergyman husband but to the society at large. In the writing too an effort was made to conceal the fact that the poems are written by a woman. The revolutionary attitude of a poet revealed in the collection as early as in the late eighties of the 19th century is a nightmare for a clergyman as well for the Australian society. A country clergyman like him cannot dream that his faithful spouse, his noble partner, could dream such thoughts, and write them and publish them.

When one read the poem *An Answer*, which is just a single poem from the collection, one realizes how ground-breaking and innovatory the piece of art is. The poems begin:

Thy love I am. Thy wife I cannot be,...

The first line introduces the theme of tradition breach, the negation to the age old tradition of marriage. Marriage is not only the oldest ritual of companionship in the society but it is also the most sacred institution and here one finds a person who is questioning the oldest and the most sanctified institution of the world.

This is a poem describing feministic philosophy as well as post colonialism at its most innovative form. The poem is feministic because it has the urge to break away the age old bondage named as marriage. It is a postcolonial poem as it voices the cry of a subaltern, a woman who wants to free herself from the repression of marital vows.

The uniqueness of the poem is the time this poem was written. It is not a joke to pen such thoughts in the late nineteenth century that too in a colonial society that was ruled by British throne and its Clergymen. More so ever the inscriber of such self-indulgent thought is a wife of a revered parish man. In this short poem Ada Cambridge has abridged the entire philosophy of feminism and that is where men had always jockeyed for place, feminists believed in rewriting the rules of the horse race. Here also Ada has tried to show how new social norms can be created to make the society a better and friendly place for the fairer sex to live.

The poem celebrates the post-colonial theory to live and let live and thus Ada writes:

But I may someday love a better man,
And thou may'st find a fitter mate than I;

The poet favours liberalism and thus she celebrates freedom. She is against all emotional and physical restraint of a woman and man both. She negates all social restrictions that cease man to behave like a human being.

The poem narrates the subjugation of women as a wife and a mate whose emotions and desires are always taken for granted. She as a human being is compelled to live a life that is a hell for her. The poem tries to show that how the regeneration of the inferior or degenerate races, by the superior races is part of the providential order of things for humanity. Here the woman is the degenerate race and marriage vows are the providential order that the woman has to maintain all lifelong whether she like it or not. And thus the poet is against all rituals of marriage that compels a human being to live a life of a bonded labour which has no choice of her own but to live a life that is guided by her lord like husband.

The poet is bold enough to call marriage as *sin-this deep and dire mistake*; marriage is sin, a mistake because according to her all human is equal and is born to live a life of her own choice. To her marriage compels a woman to live a life of slavery and bondage. She knows that marriage for most of the women is burial of her desires, expectations, aspirations and ambitions. Marriage makes a woman a slave and thus she prefers to stay with her lover but without being married because to her it is like a...*yoke of servitude*...and not only this she is daring enough to name this oldest institution as...*woman's old disgrace*.... She prefers love in return to love without giving any name to their relationship.

Ada Cambridge's greatness as a poet lies in her philosophy that brings her closer to post colonial feminist poet as she expresses her protest against the traditional marriage which are made to fulfill the need of physical or sexual enjoyment. She projects the humiliation suffered not only by the Australian but woman all over the world and this makes her a universal poet. She articulates women's liberation from bondage under male domination in one hand and on the other hand she also understands enough to write that both lover and the beloved must be given freedom to make their choices in their individual life so that their distinctiveness is maintained and thus she articulates in the last line of the poem:

> And then we must be free to kiss and part.

The poetess celebrates freedom and equality in this poem. She discards the double standard society that considers woman as a slave to her husband. She celebrates womanhood and considers woman as a comrade and helpmate of man. Her commemoration of femininity is also at the same time her condemnation for male chauvinism. To her marriage is a fake social institution where as it is love between a man and woman that is more important and so she writes:

I know thy love and love thee all I can-

The poem on the one hand condemns loveless marriage on the other it praises love, compassion and liberty. Being an Australian poet she opposes the so-called dominant ideologies of the colonial rulers and its religious heads who considers marriage and its vows as pure and unbreakable. Like any other post-colonial writers she too tries to destabilize and critically challenges the natural assumptions and the material and rational legacies of colonialism. As it is a known fact that feminism and post colonialism go together with each other rather the former is a dominant ideology of the latter; the present poem of Ada Cambridge in a way tends to represent both the ideas in a unique and genuine way.

Works Cited

Abondolo, Daniel. *A Poetics Handbook: Verbal Art in the European Tradition*. Curzon, 2001. 52-53.

Agarwal, Dauji and V.K. Gupta (Ed.). *English Literature* (UG Course Material). Agra: Vimal Prakashan, 2013. 21-22.

Habib, Rafey. *A History of Literary Criticism and Theory*. Oxford: Blackwell, 2005. 607-09, 620.

Jenkins, Lee M. Davis, Alex. (Ed.). *The Cambridge Companion to Modernist Poetry*. Cambridge: Cambridge University Press, 2007. 1-7, 38, 156.

Wimsatt, William K. Jr and Cleanth Brooks. *Literary Criticism: A Short History*. Chicago: Vintage Books, 1957. 374.

16

The Daring Exploits of Mr. Johann Ulrich Voss

Dhananjay Kumar Singh

"Whenever a new literary form appears on the scene, there are two main ways in which it can try to legitimate itself. Either it can point to its very newness as the source of its value, or it can appeal to tradition. It can claim excitedly that the world has not seen the likes of it before; or it can define what it is doing as a variation on already well-established procedures, thus hijacking some of the authorities of the past for its own purposes. In the case of the novel, the very name suggests that it is its newness which is its most striking feature" (53). Published in 1957, Patrick White's *Voss* can't be an exception to this time tested device. Critics, reviewers and of course academic readers of *Voss* have recognised its literary and aesthetic legitimacy. The novel is said to be perfectly legitimate and it can claim rightfully to be one of Patrick White's most widely read novels despite the fact that the Nobel Prize was conferred upon White for *Tree of Man* (1955). He received Miles Franklin Award for 'Voss'. The epic novel is a tribute to a great explorer who travels to unknown places in Australia in search of geographical and scientific information. Popularly known as Friedrich Ludwig Leichhardt (1813-48), he was a Prussian born Australian explorer. "In 1843, he walked 965 km/600 mi from Sydney to Moreton Bay, Queensland, and in 1844 walked from Brisbane to Arnhem Land; he disappeared during a further expedition from Queensland in 1848. Patrick

White used the character of Leichhardt in Voss". It tells the story of the 'eponymous German explorer' who sets out to map the interior of Australia, based largely on 'the real life' Ludwig Leichhardt who died in the desert in 1848.

The academic reader of Voss is overwhelmed by the positive remarks that White's scholars made in Encyclopedias and Companions. Both the cosmopolitan influence of his extensive travels and the fact that he was relatively affluent set Patrick White apart from other Australian writers, who wrote realistic novels on Australian subjects. His style which reveals the influence of James Joyce and Gertrude Stein exploits the stream of consciousness technique but is at the same time his own. He tries in his words "to find reason in apparent unreason, and how to accept a supernatural force which in one hand blesses and on the other destroys" (Benet's *Reader's Encyclopedia*, Fifth edition 2008, Harper Collins, New York, 1174).

"Voss-1957 the first part of which can be read as a fairly straight forward novel of manners, is set in Sydney in 1840s and describes preparations for the expedition into the interior of Australia. The long centred section, which employs a 'dense metaphorical style' is the story of journey itself and of how the megalomaniac explores, Voss, whose beliefs are based on Schopenhauer's theory of will, gradually comes to acknowledge humility. The first section returns to Sydney and details ironically with the making of myth of Voss, who has perished along with all the members of the expedition except one. The novel incorporates aspects of Jungian theory particularly the notions of Anima and Mandala. Voss's actual journey is complemented by the metaphorical journey of Laura Trevelyan who remains in Sydney but functions as his Anima and spiritual wife. Voss was inspired by White's reading of the Australian explorer Leichhardt and Eyre. These provided him with the starting point for an epic novel about the creation of Australian identity which also explores psychological, spiritual and gender issues (*The Cambridge Guide to Literature in English*, 2006, Cambridge, edited by Dominic Head, 1159-60).

From the mid-1950's Patrick White wrote plays, short stories and a series of epic novels which collectively attempt to configure the value of Australian society, rejecting equally the tenets of realistic writing and suburban cant: *The Tree of Man*, 1955; *Voss*, 1957; *Riders in the Chariot*, 1961; *The Solid Mandala*, 1966; and *The Vivisector*, 1970. His biographer, David Marr notes. White explorers, spinsters, dames, Jews, Spinsters Aborigines, farmers washerwomen and tramps...shake off their past to pursue a calling and reach in the end; some vision of holiness, the wonders of life (*Patrick White: A Life*, 1971). Patrick White's most studied novel, Voss tells the story of the doomed attempt of Voss to cross the Australian subcontinent describing the mystic communion that binds him to Laura who suffers with him and is released from fever at the moments of his death (*The Oxford Companion to English Literature*, Seventh Edition, 2009, Oxford, 1064).

It seems the distinguished critics while judging Patrick White's *Voss* have not yet lost sight of standards set by the Marxist critic, Terry Eagleton, 'appeal to tradition' being one among them. The Australian novel during Patrick's time was in its incipient stage. Obviously the British novel turned out to be natural choice for him. Patrick White's novels are said to be patterned after those of the British practitioners of the genre. This may be one of the reasons for employing the stream of consciousness technique in Voss. The said literary device, if we go by Eagleton's words was a 'well established procedure' to be observed in the novels of James Joyce, Virginia Woolf in Britain and by William Faukner in the U.S. Let us mark the phrase 'the likes of it before' which figures in the opening paragraph of this article. The novelist seems to be put in the dock and being interrogated by his critics thoroughly in order to prove that he is an artist of great originality. But for Patrick White's love for the Australian explorer Voss would not have seen the light of the day. The theme of romance and that of expedition are interwoven throughout the novel. The novelist makes an attempt to create Australian identity which sets him apart from his contemporaries. Characters like Voss and Laura are developed with minuteness and accuracy. Even if they appear to be ordinary, they are convincingly alive. The plot of the novel has been skilfully constructed. Life as Patrick depicts does not seem to be governed by an easy decorum. There are moments of fierce passion and deep emotion in Voss. These are some of the inferences drawn from what critics have said about the novel. The unusual features make the novel more interesting and readable. This is what Eagleton seems to have in his mind when he uses the word, 'newness'.

Vague generalizations of praise do not take us far. The novel will probably require textual analysis. Let us begin with the opening chapter of Voss set in the early nineteenth century Australia. It is a Sunday morning in New South Wales. "There is a man here, miss, asking for your uncle, said Rose. And stood breathing. What asked the young woman, who was engaged upon some embroidery of a difficult nature, at which she was now forced to look more closely, holding the little frame to the light. Or is it perhaps a gentleman" (5). Here the reader is being introduced to the protagonist of the novel who set out in search of 'your uncle'. The purpose of his visit is still unknown. Interestingly, the man is said to be a 'gentle man'. Further the 'young woman' and the so-called gentleman appear to be of a marriageable age. He is a 'foreigner and German'. Embroidery is one of the favourite past time of the woman in question who 'was most conscientious in her needle work'. Mr. Voss is the 'gentleman's name' and the young women is popularly known as Laura Trevelyan. Both meet each other on 'one of the sultry days of spring. Voss has been waiting impatiently for the last three hours at Laura's uncle's house. "You must excuse my uncle who is still at church", Laura Trevelyan said (7). During this period when the uncle is away Voss and Laura exchange pleasantries and also get down to serious discussions. He tells her how he came from Sydney on foot. This is in fact one of the daring exploits of Voss. He addresses Sydney with an easy familiarity that makes both Laura and readers feel at home. He says, "I am at home. It is like the poor parts of Germany. Sandy. It could be the Mark Brandenburg" (10). Laura replies that she had never been to Germany and found the road to Sydney monotonous, even from a carriage. She adds, "It will be sometime, I expect before I am able to grasp anything so foreign and incomprehensible. It is not my country, although I have lived in it" (11). Does it seem to belong to Voss? It does in a way. Voss, an outsider who seems to be transplanted from Germany to Australia admits, "Your country is of great subtlety" (18). But he is told by Tom Radclyfe that it is not that German's. How the Australians view their country is a serious matter and the manner in which they define nation and citizenship should be spelled out in details. Australia is a 'miserable country' according to Mrs. Bonner who is a naturalized citizen of Australia. She is one of those who accuse her husband of dragging a 'so thin' and 'already lost' fellow into expedition. But Voss enjoys the 'sultry air' he breathes in 'the new country'.

Journey is another theme that White takes up in the opening chapter of *Voss*. Mr. Bonner has just returned from church. He has 'his natural Sunday habits'. A warm welcome awaits him. Voss has been waiting for him for the 'last three quarters of an hour'. Mr. Bonner asks him if he was sure of his own ability to undertake such a 'great expedition'. Voss, a German and explorer replies that all arrangements were in hand and he had engaged four men. Nothing can break his spirit as he is in a 'fever of exploration'. We are told that it was his vocation. Also he is 'compelled into this country'.

Soon Mr. Bonner has a serious discussion with Voss on the proposed outline of the expedition including the route and the places they will visit. The places on their itinerary are Newcastle, Rhine Towers and Jildra. For this great mission Voss has recruited deserving companions such as Robarts, Le Mesuier, Palfreyman, Turner. The crew seem to have a firm and resolute determination. The merchant said, "The master of the Osprey will carry you to Newcastle, provided you are ready to embark by the date of his intended departure. There is Sanderson at Rhine Tower to see you on your way, and Boyle at Jildra which will be your last outpost, as we have decided. Each of these gentlemen has generously volunteered to contribute a mob or cattle, and Boyle, in addition, he tells me, will provide sheep as well as a considerable herd of goats. But any scientific equipment, that is your province" (20). Here the merchant assigns certain tasks to 'each of these gentle men' to be carried out conscientiously. It was a part of their job to 'contribute a mob or cattle'. The novelist says, "Still it was in his nature to play with caution" (21).

That Patrick White has introduced the theme of journey in the opening chapter of *Voss* reminds us of similar, evocative novels like Wilson Haris's *Palace of Peacock* and Joseph Conrad's *Heart of Darkness*. Here it will not be out of place to say that these novels have a strong impact upon contemporary critical thought not only in the postcolonial studies but on literary studies as well. They have engendered a considerable amount of serious debate in the 'English speaking academic communities of Europe and North America'. A critic remarks, "Palace follows in Conrad's footsteps by taking its protagonists, a mixed crew representative of the various ancestral strands of Guyanese population, or more generally of the crew of mankind, on a journey up river into the country's continental heartland. In one sense...the interior journey of Place of the Peacock retraces that of *Heart of Darkness* and there are clear Conradian echoes, for example, when the Kurtz-like protagonist, Donne remembers a house he has built 'with the closeness and intimacy of a horror and a hell and that horror and that hell he has himself elaborately constructed from which to rule the earth." It seems as if Haris were rewriting and recasting Conrad's novella. But in a way he appears to be challenging the Western literary tradition. We have a new, different in fact a 'contested vision of Africa'. Ania Loomba observes, "There in Heart of Darkness Africa is a primeval jungle and a source of power and wealth which fascinates and maddens the Colonialist hero Kurtz.... Marlow journeys down the river Congo, into the 'heart of darkness' in search of Kurtz, whose experiences are recreated as simultaneously a journey into childhood, madness and Africa. Although several critics regard Kurtz's dislocation as a product of Colonialist greed, and the novel as a critique of imperialism, it can be seen to rehearse the primitivism of classical psychoanalysis. Chinua Achebe (1989) called it a story in which the very colonialist fiction. Africa is a place where the European mind disintegrates and regresses into a primitive state" (136). What is being brought to the fore is 'the inherent rottenness of the colonial enterprise in Africa. The novel depicts Africa as 'racist'. But this is a highly controversial issue and critics are divided among themselves. According to Edward Said, one of the most distinguished Postcolonial critic there are a few problems with *Heart of Darkness* perhaps 'representational structure being one of them. The novel is said to be 'hermetic' or self enclosed. It is closed so tightly in a way that symbolically no air can go in or out. *Heart of Darkness* is impervious to external influence. Said holds, "...neither Conrad not Marlow gives us a full view of what is outside the world conquering attitudes embodied by Kurtz, Marlow, the circle of listeners on the deck of Nellie, and Conrad.... For if we cannot fully understand someone else's experience and if we must therefore depend on the assertive authority of the sort of power that Kurtz wields as a white man in the jungle or that Marlow another white man wields as a narrator, there is no use looking for other, non-imperialist alternatives; the system has simply eliminated them and made them unthinkable" (26). Does Wilson Haris's Palace seem to be trivial or vital in comparison with Conrad's *Heart of Darkness*? The comparison is still relevant to our discussion of the daring exploits of Voss. White's text reads like a 'fluid' and 'open' one where as those of Wilson and Conrad's are perfectly closed and controlled. If the politics and aesthetics as defined in *Heart of Darkness* may termed as imperialist, those in Palace should be regarded as postcolonial. These texts question not only the monolithic codes of behaviour but also open up a new vision of a developing nation. A reading of Patrick White's *Voss* shows that it can be treated as a colonialist discourse and also as a counter discourse. The novel is complex and it is open to various interpretations. The idea of land, ownership and belonging have been bequeathed to us by colonialism. Patrick White seems to suggest that European settlers should abandon their ways of thinking, create a new identity for themselves and be immersed in Australian history and culture.

Being a settler writer, Patrick White is in a situation in which a difficult choice has to be made. How to come to terms with it imaginatively? "Patrick White grew up with the impression of being permanently at a remove from Australian reality. The maxim 'only the British can be right' governed his upbringing" (205). This means Britain was a strong influence on his writings.

He is one of those who seem to have experienced alienation in Australia at a particular point of time in his life. The white Australian is treated as 'merely alien in our own land'. They are not considered to be suitable for certain purposes. One of the serious charges levelled against them is 'not oriented to the continent' and lacking a 'frame of native reference'. It will not be improper to say that a settler writer's education, literature, religious practices, cultural precepts and institutions reinforced the impression of being Britons abroad, ex-centric to what had become their native land. They seemed to be lacking meaningful connection with their surroundings. They cannot afford to lose sight of cultural roots, of home and of a sense of location. This is the reason why come across passages that shed light upon the colonial encoding of the landscape. Patrick White observes, "Wealth by colonial standards, the merchant had made his money in a solid business, out of Irish linens and Swiss muslin, damask, and huckaback, and flannel, green baize, and Indian twills. The best quality gold leaf was used to celebrate the name of EDMUND BONNER-ENGLISH DRAPER, and ladies driving down George street, the wives of officers and gazers, in barouche and brougham, would bow to that respectable man" (20). This quotation illustrates the novelist's point with the help of colonial items such as linen and muslin. The colonials saw themselves as a custodian of the public morals. The colonized were keen to emulate their colonial masters who were looked upon as a role model to be admired a great deal.

A third generation Australian, Patrick White incorporates several new colonial features into the opening chapter of *Voss*. We have with us Mr. Bonner's words. "Here we are talking about our colony as if it did not exist until now or as if it has now begun to exist as something quite different" (29). He adds, Look at our homes and public edifices. Look at the devotion of our administrators, and the solid achievement of those men who are settling the land" (20). Mr. Bonner seems to feel quite nostalgic for the place where he has been living for fairly a long stretch of time. 'Homes and public edifices' are in a way objects of veneration, thanks to his 'administrators'. The new settlers, it can be said without an iota of doubt have done a noble task.

But all is not well with the colony and it does not seem to have a great future. This worries Mr. Bonner that when and how the colony came into existence and its days of glory were numbered.

Mr. Bonner symbolizes 'the new Australian colonial bourgeoisie'. Although he adopts a rather patronizing attitude towards Voss, both are at the loggers-head over the meaning of the expedition. "If you would compare meanings, looking at each word as if it were a round pebble of mystical perfection, we would arrive perhaps at different conclusions" (20). If Voss is a born explorer, the other is a merchant. This sets Mr. Bonner apart from Voss, the German. When Mr. Bonner looks at the 'unsatisfactory map', he is curious to build on the structures of knowledge that is already 'extant' or dated. Mr. Bonner asks Voss whether the latter has seen the map which may lead them to the interior of the continent. In reply to the questions of the former, the latter however did not shrug at all. The map? Said Voss. It was certainly a vast dream from which he had wakened. Even the draper suspected its immensity as he 'prodded at the coast with his ivory pointer.' The map? Repeated the German. "I will first make it" (23). Here the map is displayed in a prominent position. A question mark hangs over the map. It is common knowledge that the map was one of most effective tools of exploitation used by colonializers. It is being consistently questioned by Voss and Mr. Bonner.

It seems to enjoy high status among colonizers. The map is a synonym for dream, colonial conventions, fantasy and a project into an overseas land. By the way who designed the map? Was it the Dutch, the French, the British or the Spanish? The map enables the colonizers to see the distant land even before they have visited it. Such a map as one of the Pacific Northwest is drawn by Jonathan Swift in Gulliver Travels. Is it possible to strip away the colonial mapping to find the essential country underneath? The colonial map is in a way a symbolic map but it functions as an actual stage or a presence in a land subjugated by the powerful nations of the world. The colonized resist the subjugation of their country. "Excluding Ireland and the 18th century experience of the United States, the white nations did not, of course, take up the weapons of political resistance. But

Australia, New Zealand and Canada (Settler or creole) writers did share with their counterparts in the decolonizing nations a desire to shake of the relationship" (204-05). A 'settler writer' like Patrick White also experiences in his own ways the cultural mimicry produced by metropolitan domination. The problem becomes more severe or serious when the migrant happens to be a Britisher, one who is transplanted from England to Australia. He may be termed as a 'White Diaspora' living on the margins of two countries. 'Englishness' is a very strong influence on their works. It is a cultural identity which is by its nature exclusive.

This was one of the reasons why F.R. Leavis does not seem to have a high opinion of Conrad. His polish origin reveals his weakness not strength. The critic writes in his *The Great Tradition*. "But Conrad was not only by far the greatest of the Edwardians; there is more to be said than that. Scott, Thackeray Meredith and Hardy are commonly accounted great English novelists: if the criterion is the achievement in work addressed to the adult mind, and capable as such of engaging again and again its full critical attention, then Conrad is a greater novelist than the four enumerated" (257). If Conrad is a distinguished author, it may be attributed to his literary out. He commands respect because of his literary acumen and achievements which reflect in his novels. But he is not among one of 'the commonly accounted great English novelists'. The country of origin does matter as Leavis puts it in a way. Englishness/inwardness, it can be said refers to the modern British identity.

A nation signifies people who share a culture, history, a language, a homeland and a shared sense of the self. This seems to be one of the ways in which Englishness has been promoted and celebrated. Is 'pure English'/'true English' a myth to be challenged? Should it be taken to mean that Englishness is a racial and ethnic identity or Englishness has to do with a sense of belonging to one's dwelling place? That, is England for the English. Things change with the passage of time. Today we have a multicultural dimension of Englishness which invalidates in a way Leavis's version of Englishness. He perhaps meant by Englishness a commitment and a sense of belonging to England. It is quite possible to be in England and not be remotely English.

Thus Englishness suggests in a way the moral and cultural superiority of Britain and Britishers as an exponent of the myth of the White Man's burden.

Britishers as settlers in Australia do not have a different story to narrate and Patrick White, the author of *Voss*, *Riders in a Chariot*, *Tree of Life*, etc. He was not only born in London but also studied in King's College, Cambridge University. It is very difficult to say whether his experiences in Australia were similar to those of the colonized indigenous people or he was at a distance from them. Ania Loomba observes, "White settlers were historically the agents of the colonial rule, and their subsequent development—cultural as well as economic—does not simply align with their colonized peoples...white population were here not subject to genocide, economic exploitation, cultural decimation and political exclusion felt by indigenous people" (140). In historical parlance the idea of anti-colonial struggle and demand for independence has dawned upon Australians very late. They also gave up the idea of snapping their ties with the British Commonwealth in the late twentieth century. The Australians seems to have a close relationship with Britain which is often stated as that of margin to the centre.

When we focus on the representation of colonialism and imperialism in literature in general and White's *Voss* in particular, we are always reminded of Conrad's *Heart of Darkness*. The early critic of Colonialism notes, "The conquest of the earth, which mostly means taking it away from those who have a different complexion or slightly flatter noses than ourselves, is not a pretty thing when you look into two much. What redeems it is the idea only, an idea at the back of it, not a sentimental pretence but an idea, and an unselfish belief in the idea-something you can set up, and bow down before, and offer a sacrifice to" (24). Here Conrad describes Marlowe's visit to the interiors of Congo where he meets Mr. Kurtz. The reader is made aware of the problems inherent in imperialism and colonialism. Despite 'The conquest of the earth' by Colonial masters, the colonized/the savage do not have a sense of being enlightened. Government and trading centres are some of institutions established by the European colonizers and imperialists. As this was not enough, they invaded fought and provoked endless wars. There seemed to be a profit motive for colonial projects. Marlow saw a ship that fired indiscriminately into a jungle. Such an act as one described above symbolizes futility and destruction that accompany Colonialism and imperialism. The invaders establish an infrastructure of government, trade, hospitals and education for the noble savage. But they could not stop themselves from indulging in the theft of the local wealth. They collected precious metals and enslaved the indigenous people whom they describe as primitive savage.

Conrad's *Heart of Darkness* forms a dramatic backdrop to Patrick White's *Voss*. Let us concentrate on the opening chapter of the novel. One notes that one of the ways of opening the text is through the deployment of 'peritexts' like titles, subtitles, dedications, notices and so on. Patrick White's *Voss* is particularly notable for its title. The novel is one of character and the character in question is no other than *Voss*. A man of character, he has been portrayed by the novelist as a 'german', 'crag of man', 'cloudy', 'shaby', 'uncouth' 'nasty', 'old', 'disreputable subject', etc. "Voss was a bit of scarecrow. He was a bit mad" (26). The common reader would like to know the values that Voss aspires for and also the kind of motive force and radical attitude that can give meaning, direction and coherence to life. He/she remembers certain remarks of T.S. Eliot with pride and honour. "A living character is not necessarily 'true to life'. It is a person whom we can see and hear, whether he be true or false to human nature as we know it. What the creator of the character needs is not so much knowledge of motives as keen sensibility; the dramatist need not understand people, but he must be exceptionally aware of them" (224).

It will be seen in course of a brief perusal of Voss that the keen sensibility and the exceptional awareness become apparent to us. His daring exploits arouse our curiosity in him. He does something unusual and brave in diverse spheres of life. Patrick White tells us about his deeds while he is travelling in Australia. It seems as if 'by right of vision' he were born in Australia not in Germany and Australia would be his motherland. A sense of belonging and a commitment to the nation sets him apart from a Kurtz or a Marlow. Voss is strong, brave, determined and difficult to be defeated or frightened. Indomitably cheerful, he would continue to make explorations of Australia and the human heart. "He does not intend to make a fortune out of this country, like other men. He is not all money talk" (28). These are the words of his fiancé, Laura who knows from experience that Voss would ride very far into it. Australia is a 'country of the future'. It is also known as a land of opportunities. But Voss's intention is not to make a huge fortune from his visit to Australia. "Some pitied him. Some despised him for his funny appearance of a foreigner. None, he realized with a tremor of anger, was conscious of his strength. Mediocre, animal men never do guess at the power of rock of fire, until the last moment before these elements reduce them to...nothing" (Chapter 3). Friends of Voss despise him for reasons best them to themselves. Perhaps 'His funny appearance of a German' was one of the causes. A few could take notice of his strength and speak high of his abilities.

Voss reads like a travelogue. It seems the physical typography or the geographical awareness of Australia did not matter much to the writer. He was in a way imbued with a desire for something strange. Romanticism had a profound impact on him. The theme of journey is said to be quite experimental in character. It is a kind of self-discovery. The progress through the land is a journey into one's self. Voss's visit to New South Wales Voss provides him with an opportunity to have a 'mimetic version of the original homeland' that settlers like Mr. Bonner have left behind himself. Mr. Bonner is one of them who has been transplanted from England to Australia. The newly discovered land chants him as much as it does to Voss, the German explorer. It will not be unfair to say that Australia is incredibly romantic country. The nation has a wide appeal. There is a note about the hidden aspect of romanticism in Voss's journey made by Patrick White's biographer, David Marr. "The first stage of Voss's journey takes the party by the sea to Newcastle and overland through the gentle, healing landscape of the hunter to Rhine Towers...Rhine Towers in the case of the Sandersons—is a place of simplicity and perfection, an Eden in the bush.... Voss leads the party from that sublime valley across New England to the flat coolabahs country.... West of Jildra lies the desert. Once the expedition left Jildra, Voss was on an expedition to the outer limits of his imagination" (50). The beauty of the passage lies in the romantic landscape. The reader can see the river, 'the bush', 'the desert', 'the valley', 'the sea' and so on when he/ she looks across Australia. He is in a position to address places such as Newcastle and Rhine Towers with an easy familiarity that makes him feel at home. Further these places seem to be 'sublime' and also they denote 'simplicity' and 'perfection'. Here the imagery from the natural world suggest romantic connotation. Imagination is one of them. It seems to be one of the chief attributes of Voss's personality. His exploits are really exciting and stretch the imagination beyond its limit. If we go by David Marr's account of Voss's journey into the strange and romantic interior of Australia, our observation is the journey occurs on a straight line rather on a curve. But the protagonist cannot avoid confronting nature that seems to threaten him or appears to be difficult to deal with.

Patrick White's treatment of Nature in Voss shows it is treated with more respect by the aboriginals. The whites on the other hand behave reasonably well. They have a garden with flowers, plants and vegetables. On weekends they spend their time in it. Gardening seems to be the favourite past time of Mr. Bonner's family. Laura tells Voss about her uncle's love for the garden. Here both of them sit together and share pleasantries. Like the river or a lake the garden does not occur naturally. It has been created by man with the help of science and technology. Patrick White contrasts the situation then with the dense primeval forests that cover the interior of Australia. Eye-witness accounts of Nature in Jildra differ markedly from those of New South Wales. "By now the tall grass was almost dry, so that there issued from it a sharper sighing when the wind blew. The wind bent the grass into tawny waves, on the crests of which floated the last survivor of flowers, and shrivelled and were sucked under by the swell. All day the horses and cattle swam through this grass sea. Their barrels rolled and gurgled. All night the beasts were glutting themselves on due and grass, but in the dreams of men the waves of grass and the waves of sleep were soon one" (165). That the reader of Voss is 'in the vicinity of Jildra' can be shown by providing evidences from nature. The novelist's power of description merits attention. It contains description as well as discussion of the issues involved in the journey. White creates a dark and gloomy atmosphere. The 'grass' is said to be 'tall' but completely dry. This is contrary to the popular belief that grass is a common wild plant with green leaves. The grass does not sing. Rather it sighs. It appears as if it were expressing feelings of disappointment. Something unpleasant might happen to Voss. The 'wind' turned violent and therefore 'bent the grass' which looked like 'waves' of brownish and yellow colour. The writer gives us a pictorial record of the expedition. Certain phrases such as 'the last survivor', 'waves of grass' and 'waves of sleep' suggest that White has noticed something untoward. He realizes the fact that Voss will be in deep trouble. The disaster cannot be averted.

Nature in Jildra holds a fascination for students of literature on the both sides of the Atlantic. The moon is an important attraction. It appears and disappears in the sky. A beautiful moon lit night makes us extremely happy and excited. But the moon does not always seem to have connotation of happiness and indulgence. Time and again the moon is at the back of the novelist's mind. Patrick White writes, "Heavy moons hung above Jildra at that season. There was a golden moon, of placid, swollen belly. There was the ugly bronze, male moons, threateningly lopsided. One night of wind and dust, there was a pale moonstone, or as rags of clouds polished its face, delicate glass instrument, on which the needle barely fluttered, indicating the direction that some starry destiny must take. The dreams of men were influenced by the various moons, with the result that they were burying their faces in the pregnant moon-woman, or shaking their bronze fists at any threat to their virility. Their dreams eluded them, however, under the indicator of that magnetic moon" (176). At this point the writer seems to convey an idea of the 'predicament' of the characters of the novel. Life is in a way all gloom and despondency. Is there any suggestions about how best to tackle the problem? Perhaps the moon in the plural is willing to respond to this question. Some of its features the novelist has noted in the above-mentioned passage are 'heavy', 'golden', 'placid', 'male', 'pale', etc.

Let us shift our emphasis from treatment of nature to the idea of time in Voss. We find a correspondence between nature and time. There is a linear relationship between nature and time. The narrative progresses in a straight line. In fact, it begins in Spring. "It was one of the sultry days of Spring, the young woman was dabbing at her upper lip with a handkerchief as she waited" (9). The novelist observes, "One evening that spring when the street was already dissolving and amiable pedestrian were calling to one another in friendship" (11). Voss comes into contact with Laura in spring. They become lovers soon after they first met in Spring in New South Wales. Spring is a beautiful season. The weather becomes warmer. Plants start to grow again. Many flowers bloom. We notice the distinctive changes in the season that follow a cyclic pattern in the novel. Voss leaves New South Wales for Jildra. His observations on life in Jildra are recorded in these words. "Written words take some time to thaw but the words of Lilies were now flowing in full summer water, whether it was the water or the leaves of water, and dark hairs of roots plastered on the mouth as water blew across" (187). This passage gives us all the relevant information about seasons. It is summer in Jildra. Voss and his party have already drawn an outline for their journey and they proceed. On the way, they are swept by 'intermittent showers of rain'. Further, it is important to consider the role of the season. How long does the dry/hurricane/spring season last? We can infer that Voss and his party got caught in the torrential rain. In all likelihood it was a rainy season. The beauty of the romantic landscape of the novel lies in the fact that it leads us to three typographical variables—land, water and the desert apart from nature and the seasonal cycle. We may view Voss as an attempt of the novelist to link the past with future. Time and space are usually intended to interact with each other in fiction. A critical reading of Voss enables us to move from New South Wales to New Castle and then to Jildra. The natural seasons—spring, summer and rainy look equally nice to us. One of the reasons is that time and space move in a linear directions. This accounts for the increasing popularity of the novel.

In his preoccupation with the past, Patrick White has enriched our understanding of life and its mysteries. The major characters of Voss seem to be 'apprenticed to the past'. "So the past now swelled in distorting bubbles, like the windows of the warehouse in which his father an old man, gave orders to apprentices and clerks, and the sweet smell of blond timber suggested all safety and virtue" (13). What is Patrick White driving at now? It seems the author is eulogizing the past. He is certainly steeped in the rich tradition of Australia. He draws an analogy between the 'past' and 'warehouse' which is a kind of reservoir of 'safety' and 'virtue' for Mr. Bonner and the like. The garden episode in chapter four gives us a sense of the past but it is different from the one that we see in the first chapter of the novel. Laura experiences herself 'threatening to disintegrate into the voices of the past'. She and Voss are ordained by heaven to 'fill the great gap of space and time'. Their awareness of future increases dramatically. "Future is will". Ludlow asks Laura when the future 'becomes' the present. Her response is quite encouraging. That is, 'now'. She seems to have extraordinary powers of perception for life. "Every moment that we live and breathe, and love, and suffer and die" (120). The real test of her mettle came in the wake of premature death of Voss. "Voss did not die. He is there still, it is said, in the country, and always will be". Here is a linear perspective of life reflecting as it does in Laura. The manner in which she blends the past (did) with the present (is) and future (will) suggests time cannot be fragmented into three equal parts. Time is a long continuum. Even if it changes in character gradually or in slight stages, it does so without any clear dividing points.

It is not easy to discern some pattern in Patrick White's *Voss*. The use of dreams and visions make the novel difficult to understand. Dreams and visions are not considered to be a part of realistic mode of presentation. They in fact, go into the making of the stream of consciousness novel. Dreams and visions are a recurring motif in Voss. The protagonist reads, or 'dreams aloud' in his native language: "Am blassen Meeresstrande...naher and naher..." (81). These words are barely comprehensible to Mrs. Bonner as they are German and not English. A fat or reduced version of the text may not look like the original. This is what Voss means when he is asked by Mrs. Bonner to explain the meaning of the text. He says, "Poetry will not bear translation. It is too personal" (81). Should it be taken to mean that there is a definite edge in poetry when it is compared with prose? Here the novelists talks about the risks inherent in translation. He loves poetry because it is written from personal experience and it deals with one's own self.

The following extract from chapter five of *Voss* is about dream. In response to the Sailor's yearn Palfreyman says, "If it happened in a dream that was not distinguishable from life, it is still a matter for your conscience. You wished to live what you dreamt" (97). We have a dream while we are asleep. We often think about it because we would like it to happen. With White we learn the meaning of dream. The real importance of dream can be felt when we hear these words of the sailor. "But if it happened, he continued and began to be consoled, if it happened that a woman really had a part in it, then she was as much to blame, and never making so much as a sign. If the woman took part in it, Palfreyman said. She must be a bad woman. But in a dream? The sailor mused" (97). Let us read the given passage carefully. We find it contains a subordinate clause (But if it happened) which occurs twice. It seems to collocate well with dream. Is it an English collocation or do we need to be aware of its wider implications in terms of Freud's seminal essay, "The Interpretation of Dreams"? The third person narrator describes not only his mode of dreaming but also that of others. If the action of dreaming itself is syncretic, that is, a fusion of different meanings, then objects can also dream and may be read as symbolic, as having visionary significance or as a mystical notion of the influence of landscape on the human psyche. Such a reading of Patrick White's *Voss* does not stray away from its positioning as a colonial text. It offers a glimpse of colonial Sydney. This is one of the dominant issues that run through the first part of the novel. Sydney looks like a small place. The countryside is still a part of the town. The public roads in Sydney that has houses and shops on both sides are a few. The reader may go for a stroll in the streets and have the impression that Sydney is an ancient city with a colonial past. People seem to be doing well. But they bask in the admiration of colonial Englishness/'inwardness' as Patrick White puts them. Colonel Featurestoodhaugh's speech delivered at the farewell reads like a sermon on Colonialism:

> Indeed when a space had been cleared, he made a speech, about God and soil and flag and our Young Illustrious Queen, as had been prepared for him. The numerous grave and appreciative persons who were surrounding the Colonel lent weight to his appropriate words. These were for instance, at least three members of the Legislative council, a Bishop, a Judge, officers in the Army, besides patrons of the expedition, and citizens whose wealth had begun to make them acceptable, in spite of their unfortunate past and persistent clumsiness with knife and fork. Important heads were bared; stiff necks were bent into attitudes that suggested humble attention.
>
> It was a brave sight, and suddenly also moving. For all those clothes of figure and linen, of worthy flesh alone and the souls tied to them, temporarily, like tentative balloons, by the precious grace of life, might, of that sudden, have been cardboard or little wooden things, as their importance in the scene receded, and there predominated the great tongue of blue water, the brooding indigenous trees, and the sky clutching at all (113). This passage shows that during colonial period acceptability did not convey the same meaning as respectability. A rigid hierarchy of social classes (Bishop, judge, officers in the army) is also being emphasized. The novelist seems to have made a strong argument for 'Englishness'/'inwardness', a natural corollary of Colonialism and imperialism. Attitudinal changes are noticeable with the passage of time. The colonial masters have to deal with many challenges to their authority, nature being one of them. It will not be out of place to put on record Laura's observations. She seems to be keenly aware of the problem. She says, "I am uncomfortably aware of the very little I have seen and experienced of things in general and of our

country in particular. Quite the reverse, it overflows all maps that exist. Perhaps true knowledge comes of death by torture in the country of the mind" (51). Ever one knows that the map was one of the weapons used by colonizers for their territorial gains. Let's mark Laura's words 'overflows' which suggests remarkable changes in Australian society. This may be the first step in the assertion of Independence/national identity.

One has to digress so often while writing an article that sometimes it is difficult to follow what is being said because it is different from the main subject being discussed. If allowed to digress for the moment, one would like to briefly mention the earlier role played by dreams and visions in Patrick White's *Voss*. Being an accomplished artist, the protagonist has fecund imagination. He is really dreamy and as much as his fiancé is. Voss and Palfreyman speak to each other before both are leaving Jildra. The latter makes a beautiful sketch which strikes a personal chord with the former. The Australian lily makes an immediate impact on Voss, and he expresses his emotions in a very powerful manner. "Written words take some time to thaw but the words of lilies were now flowing in full summer water, and dark hairs of roots plastered on the mouth as the water blew across.... Tear out the black thing by the roots before it has taken hold. She was humbly grateful for it, however. In her kneeling position, she continues to bathe her hair in all flesh, whether of imperial lilies, or the black, putrefying human kind" (183). The passage contains echoes of English romantic poets. There seems to be something Wordsworthian about it. The outpourings of Voss's heart have an inter textual link with Wordsworth's 'Ode on Intimations of Immortality'.

To me the meanest flower that blows can give

Thoughts that do often lie too deep for tears. (306)

Laura says that she is not purely romantic. When Voss's ship, Osprey leaves for its destination, she undergoes a dreamy experience. "But the dream persisted disturbingly. Laura Trevelyan, drawing back her lips to bite the slice of bread and honey, saw whole rows of sailors' blackened teeth gaping from a gunnel. The knife with which she slashed. The knife with which she slashed the butter, had a mottled, slippery handle and could have been made from horse's hoof" (119). What is immediately apparent to us is a fact that Laura is dreamy. A kind of 'feverish melancholy' begins to 'take possession' of her. Is it the 'ship with its evident furiness' or 'such a sight' that worry her about something (black teeth). She looks a little perturbed. "The whole row of sailors" nearly frightens the life out of her. She is extremely afraid of a 'gunnel'. Who knows the boat of her life may capsize in heavy seas. She has a premonition of death that Voss was in real danger. This may be one of the reasons why Patrick White points to 'gunnel'. That is, the upper edge of the side of the boat. As a matter of fact, when a boat turns over, it is the upper part which is the first to be covered with water completely.

Voss is replete with dreams. The ominous presence of a dreadful snake in Le Mesurier's dream that occurs in the 10th chapter of the novel suggest that he was in a way aware of the danger from unknown forces. As Voss parted ways with the band, Laura had fits of delirium. But what she said in a state of extreme excitement made some sense. "I shall not fail you". Even though she is separated from Voss, she can still remain united with him. Voss also had a vision in which Laura appeared. He imagined, "Then he looked at her, and saw that they had cut off her hair, and below the surprising stubble that remained, they had pared the flesh from her face. She was quite naked and beautiful" (383). 'The fond and wayward thoughts' which come into his mind affirm his remarkable affinity with Laura. Both of them liked and understood each other. There seemed to be a close relationship between the two.

The fate of a romantic relationship seems to at the centre of this poignant, novel. It ultimately has to say a number of things about the nature of romantic love. According to Patrick White, *Voss* is a story of 'grand passion'. Love grows in the minds of Voss and Laura. If they feel drawn towards each other, they owe it to nature. No one can doubt her love for Voss. The 'German is just a lonely man looking for love, for someone who can lend a helping hand to him. She adores Voss because he looks for adventures. He is one of those who likes dangers or exciting experiences. Laura seems to have a lot of sympathy for him. That's why he holds her in esteem. Both do not meet regularly. They see each other on three or four occasions before the absorbing voyage of discovery is made. Also Voss and Laura have a very strong feeling of dislike for certain things. As time passes, they think about the cosy intimacy they had shared. Voss proposes her out of vanity and Laura does so 'out of a desire to save him from his delusions of divinity'. One thinks that romantic love has been given a serious treatment in the novel. The novelist is also aware of the subtle nuances of love. He defines love as a psychic/spiritual experience. What does love mean in concrete terms? Is love a pure abstraction? The novelist addresses himself to the task of searching a new meaning of love. The light shade in love is often contrasted with the dark one. The following passage can be used to explain the above-mentioned argument. "Or, she closed her eyes, and they rode northward together between the small hills, some green and soft, with the feathers of the young corn ruffled on their sides, others hard and blue as sapphires. As the two visionaries rode, their teeth were shivering, flashing, for their faces anonymous with love, was turned naturally towards each other, and they did from time to time, catch such irrelevantly personal glimpses. What they were saying had not yet been translated out of air, the rustling of the corn, and the resilient cries of the birds. As they rode on, all metal was twinning together of stirrup-irons for instance and the bits of the mouths of their horses" (167). This passage assesses the significance of love in the life of Voss and Laura. Both are described as 'two visionaries'. There is a constant repetition of the same clause, "they rode". They are still riding high after their meeting in the garden. They seem to be defined by their faces anonymous with love. Whatever step they take has to do with the preservation of anonymity and they wish to remain 'unseen' and 'unknown'.

There is however another passage in *Voss* which throws light on elements of love—love as an abstraction. The novelist uses strange images and sounds to convey the hallucinatory reactions of lovers. Their love for each other cause them to hallucinate an oasis in a desert. The desert, it can be said is a recurring motif in *Voss*. "So he rode through hell, until he felt her touch him. I shall not fail you, said Laura. Even if there are times when you are with me to, I shall not fail you. He will not look at her, however, for he was not yet ready.... You are not in the possession of your faculties, he said to her at last. What are my faculties? She asked. Then they were drifting together. They were sharing the same hell, in their common flesh, which he had attempted so often to repudiate. She was fitting him with a sheath of tender white" (119). Here we seem to be monitoring the activities of lovers as they 'ride'. Neither Laura nor Voss wants to disappoint each other. This is meant by the expression, 'I shall not fail you' which occurs twice. The voice of lovers does not lack conviction. In fact, they are motivated by deep religious feelings. Being 'not in the possession of one's faculties' reveals the strength and not the weakness or a disability which limits the physical or mental abilities of a person and more so when it concerns Laura. She is 'sharing the same hell' with Voss. Do they conform to approved standards of romance? If they do, then love should not be termed as 'hell'. There is no need to 'repudiate' the values of the past. May be the novelist says one thing and means the opposite. He has in his mind heaven or pure bliss when he uses the word, 'hell'.

Voss and Laura are destined to live apart. The eventual separation causes us to pause and reflect. David Marr, a Patrick White Scholar has something in this regard to offer. "As the two characters are separated by events and distances, their stories have to be developed alternatively, but they also fuse, in dreams, in memories and in delirium—most closely, for instance, when Voss is lying half dead of thirst and starvation, and Laura is suffering from delusions as a result of a psychic disturbance diagnosed as the inevitable brain fever. Voss is finally dragged through the dust, and accepts the principles Laura would have liked him to accept before he is murdered by the blacks. Laura recovers. She becomes a head mistress and a figure of some respect in the community, if also one that nobody really understands, because of some mysterious past" (314). Where and how does Voss live? We know his whereabouts. 'Dreams, memories, delirium' and of course the letters which Voss and

Laura write to each other are our sources of information. Here is Voss in his own words, "Dear Miss Trevelyan, do not pray for me, but I would ask you to join me in thought and exercise of will, daily, hourly, and exercise of will, daily, hourly, until I may return to you, the victor" (153). The information has been given by Voss who is directly involved in the affair. The veracity of the account can not be questioned. It is largely supported by David Marr.

Voss's letter reaches its 'destination'. Laura replies with a smile on her face. "So, Mr. Voss we have reached a stage where I am called upon to consider my destroyer as my saviour! I must take on trust those tender feelings you profess, and which I cannot trace clearly the labyrinth of our relationship. Can you wonder that I am confused? All the more since I have remained morbidly sensitive to the welfare of one whose virtues do not outweigh the many faults I have continued to despise" (185). Here we have nothing but praise for Voss from Laura. She steals a covert glance at him across the desert where he is longing for 'the welfare of one' which can turn him into a 'victor'. It seems to be paradoxical that her destroyer is her Saviour. To destroy and to save are said to be opposite features and therefore they appear to be strange. This question has been answered by Voss. "To make yourself, it is necessary to destroy yourself" (34). Laura does not 'conceal her opinions'. She says, "Arrogance is surely the quality that cause us to recognize each other. Nobody within my memory, I have realized since dared so much as to disturb my pride, except in Puppyish ways. Men, I am inclined to think, are frightened if there self-importance does not impress" (185). Laura describes the circumstances in which she comes into contact with Voss. It is a strange coincidence that arrogance brings Voss and Laura together. She also makes a strong political statement on men. Suffice to say that of the two—man and woman—it is woman who can be said to be more aware of her insignificance and isolation as Laura puts it. The reader has not seen the possible outcome of 'their mutual hatefulness' and 'wretched failures'. Laura remarks, "And have you not, perhaps mistaken a critical monster for a compliant mouse?" (186).

It is not the theme or plot that contributes greatly to the success of Patrick's writing style in Voss. An analysis of the language, symbols and imagery can result in new insights, which can help us in coming to a new interpretation of the text. Voss is not merely an explorer of the new continent. That is, Australia. He is keenly interested in the 'labyrinth of human relationship. Like a poet he has given the emotional rendering of his feelings in terms of a metaphor. Voss wants to ascertain the fact how much she loves him. She answers his question. "I am fascinated by you. You.... You are my desert!" (88). She trusts him while equating him with a desert. This seems to be a frank admission on the part of Laura. The statement has been made in a rare moment of candour. By no stretch of imagination it can be termed as 'immodest'. Laura further says, "You are so vast and ugly. I can imagine some desert, with rocks, rocks of prejudice, and yes even hatred. You are so isolated. That is why you are fascinated by the prospect of desert places. In which you find your own situation taken for granted, or more than that, exalted" (87).

But how does Voss reciprocate Laura's gesture of love. Patrick White speaks on behalf of Voss. "From where he was standing, he could watch the secret place at the nape of her neck, of infinite creaminess, and the swathe of greeny-white veil round the hard, dark crown of her hat. He had never yet dared to touch, except through those formal gestures society expects, or else, the formless, self-explanatory liberties of sleep. Human relationships are as vast as deserts: they demand all daring" (192). Here is a direct communication from the novelist to the reader about Voss without speaking to him. Similar suggestions about Voss have been made by Laura. The image of a desert begins to appear before us. It has enormous symbolic significance. It stands for the vastness of space in Australia. It also shows magnanimity. Voss and Laura have a kind and generous nature. They do not resent to what other characters in the novel have said and done to them.

What does Patrick White keep beneath the image of desert? It is remarkably difficult to answer this question. The metaphor contains undertones of a metaphysical poem, "To His Coy Mistress" by Andrew Marvell.

But at my back I always hear
Time's winged chariot hurrying near;
And yonder all before us lie
Deserts of vast eternity. (300)

This stanza reads like a carpe deim. Here the lovers want to live fully each moment of their life in a heroic defiance of Time's slow chapped power. 'Times winged chariot' is the traditional metaphor for the vehicle in which the sun, moon, night and time are represented as pursuing their course. Like Marvell's lovers, those of Patrick White are conscious of the brevity of youth and life, mutability and morality and time and space continuum. The desert arch type in Marvell's poem has been presented as another kind of time to be contrasted with 'Had we but world enough time' of the first stanza of the poem and time, "This coyness, Lady, were no crime" (299). The desert represents the age old dilemma of 'time and immortality'. "If life is to be judged not by duration but by intensity, then Marvell's lovers at least during the act of love will achieve a kind of immortality by devouring time or by transcending the laws of clock time (Time's Winged Chariot)" (175). But the contrary is true for Voss and Laura. Their's is a classic case of unrequited love.

If we examine the literary form of Voss, we note it is a novel of epic proportions. The novel seems to have achieved the status of an epic, thanks to the daring exploits of Voss. Historically speaking, "epic elements are incorporated into the eighteenth century novel through the device of the Picaresque, especially the motif of the journey as it occurs in Gulliver's *Travels* and again in Stern's *Sentimental Journey*" (142). Heroism is also democratised in Patrick White's *Voss* which bears a striking resemblance to Homer's *Illiad*. One thinks that the parallelism between these two novels does not amount to exaggeration. The opening chapter of Voss reminds us of Voss's collection of certain adventures. In *Illiad*, we come across an assembly of Achaean soldiers. Homer writes in Book 1, Achilles and Agamemnon.

You Kings and Warriors! May your vows be crowned
And Troy's proud wall lie level with the ground.
May Jove restore you when your tools are over

Safe to the pleasures of your native shore.
But oh! Relieve a wretched parent's pains
And give Chrysies to these arms again;
If mercy fails, yet let my presents move,
And dread avenging Phoebus, Son of Jove. (5)

Illiad opens with Homer's invocation to the muse of poetry. In his invocation the poet states his theme—the wrath or the anger of Achilles. He requests the Moses to inspire him so that he can narrate the story.

Coming to the parallelism between *Voss* and *Illiad* again. 'Vastness of the epic battle' is similar to that of Voss's journey. Difference between Achilles and Agamemnon and Difference between Voss and Turner cannot be said to be entirely different from each other.' Achilles's withdrawal from the Myrmidons' and withdrawal of Turner and others with Judd as the leader reinforces in a way parallelism between Illiad and Voss. The former contains Lacoon and the snake which point to a decisive finality. The snake in the latter performs similar functions. Illiad ends on a note of pessimism in the wake of death and destruction. So does Voss. There is a series of death in the novel.

Towards the end of the novel the reader wants to know whether he/she should admire the behaviour and attitudes of the mutiniers who failed to help Voss. He was relying entirely on them. Credit goes to the brave fighters for accomplishing a dream. They had laid down their lives for a serious cause. When Laura meets Judd, one of the 'deserters' she learns that Judd's wife and children had died before he arrived. Finally who is greater? There seems to be a general consensus among readers about Voss's greatness. He dies in a heroic manner. Laura in a tribute to him says, "Voss did not die. He is there still, it is said in the country and always will be. His legend will be written down, eventually, by those who have been troubled by it" (448). Voss was a legend in his own life time. One of the reasons was he had the ability to think about or plan the future with great imagination and intelligence. He said, "The mystery of life is not solved by success, which is an end in itself, but in the failure, in perpetual struggle, in becoming" (71).

Thus, Patrick White's *Voss* is more than a dramatization of the daring exploits of Voss against a colonial back drop. The novelist paints a compelling picture of Australia. The theme of identity has been explored in a comprehensive and stimulating manner. Written from the third person point of view, Voss is an arresting, devastating and visual novel. It is an unforgettable picture of Australians in the midst of extraordinary times. Patrick White remains today one of the best and most interesting author of his generation. Few Australian writers now can match his narrative poise and he seems to be peerless in his articulation of the unspoken. A brilliant stylist, he delves unflinchingly into the enduring mysteries of life.

References

Boehmer, Elleke. *Colonial and Post Colonial Literature*. Migrant Metaphors, Second Edition. New York: Oxford University Press, 2005. 204-05.

Conrad, Joseph. *Heart of Darkness*. Mumbai: Orient Longman, 2003. 24.

Eagleton, Terry. *The English Novel*. Oxford: Blackwell Publishing, 2005. 53.

Greenblatt, Stephen and M.H. Abrams. *The Norton Anthology of English Literature*, Volume-D. The Romantic Period. New York and London: W.W. Norton & Company, 2006. 306.

Guerin, Wilfred L., Farle G. Labour and Morgan, Willingham. *A Handbook of Critical Approaches to Literature*, Second Edition. New York: Harper & Row Publishers, 1979. 175, 299-300.

Innes, Paul. *Epic*. London: Routledge, 2013. 142.

Leavis, F.R. *The Great Tradition*. London: Faber & Faber, 1988. 224, 257.

Loomba, Ania. *Colonialism/Postcolonialism*. London and New York: Routledge, 2000. 136, 140.

Marr, David. *Patrick White: A Life*. Victoria: Random Century, 1991. 50, 314.

Rieu, E.V. *D.C.H. Rieu*. London: Penguin, 1991. 5.

Said, Edward W. *Culture and Imperialism*. London: Vintage, 1994. 26.

The Wordsworth Encyclopedia, Volume. 3 gril-microm. Hertfordshire: Wordsworth Edition Limited, 1995. 1264.

Thiem, John. *Post-Colonial Contexts: Writing Back to the Canon*. London and New York: Continuum, 2001. 27.

Index